ISBN 1-930596-28-6

Published by THE GUEST COTTAGE, INC.
PO Box 848
Woodruff, WI 54568
1-800-333-8122

www.theguestcottage.com

Designed and marketed by The Guest Cottage Inc.
Cover art by Kathleen Parr McKenna of McKenna Design

Printed in Canada

The Guest Cottage Inc.
dba Amherst Press

# Cooking Inn Style

## bon Appétit!

*Recipes from the*

*Innkeepers of the Wisconsin*

*Bed & Breakfast Association*

*Bon Appétit* – *"good appetite, the desire for the health and happiness of someone about to have a meal"* is our wish to you! The innkeepers of the Wisconsin Bed & Breakfast Association present their bona fide recipes in these pages, to be enjoyed at our table or at your table. This is the sixth cookbook by WBBA.

**Wisconsin Bed & Breakfast Association**

**www.wbba.org**

**the right place to find the right place!**

**Search by the amenities you desire...**

**find the perfect B&B for your 'bon voyage'!**

# Contents

# Participating Inns

# Guide By City of Participating Inns

# *State Map of Participating Inns*

Bayfield

Ashland

Florence

Eagle River

Crandon

Osceola  Turtle Lake

Holcombe

Sister Bay

Ephraim

Hudson  Chippewa Falls

Menomonie

Wausau

Baileys Harbor

Sturgeon Bay

Stevens Point

Waupaca

Appleton

Green Lake

Westfield

Sparta

Portage  Pardeeville

La Crosse

Westby

Plymouth  Sheboygan

La Farge  Reedsburg

Sheboygan Falls

Mayville

Richland Center  Baraboo  Horicon

Port Washington

Blue River  Lodi  Fall River

Spring Green

Mequon

Madison

Wauwatosa

Belleville  Fort Atkinson

New Glarus  Whitewater

Albany  Burlington

Lake Geneva

5

# Oak Hill Manor
# Bed & Breakfast

**401 East Main Street**
**Albany, WI 53502**
**(608)862-1400**
**www.oakhillmanor.com**
**innkeeper@oakhillmanor.com**

*Hosts: Gene & Barbara Tolli*

Oak Hill Manor has four sunny corner bedrooms, all with private baths. Choose a room with a fireplace, canopy bed, enclosed porch with wicker furniture, or a claw-foot tub. We sponsor "ladies midweek" getaways from February through June, which are a welcome reprieve for many of our guests.

Albany is a village nestled on the Sugar River within two hours of the Chicago area, Milwaukee, and Iowa. Enjoy biking the Sugar River Trail, canoeing and golfing. Come and enjoy the perfect blend of elegance and comfort.

*Rates at Oak Hill Manor range from $85 to $105.*
*Rates include a full breakfast.*

# Individual Strawberry/Rhubarb Crisps with raspberry syrup

*This wonderful recipe won second place in the dessert category at the Food For Thought Festival in Madison. All fruits come from local Wisconsin farms.*

Serves 6

*Crisps:*
- 12 ounces fresh rhubarb, trimmed and cut into 1/2" pieces
- 12 ounces fresh strawberries, stems removed and hulled, sliced
- 1/3 cup sugar or less, depending on the sweetness of your strawberries
- 2 Tablespoons all-purpose flour
- 1/2 teaspoon grated orange rind
- 1/2 teaspoon ground cinnamon
- 1/3 teaspoon nutmeg

*Streusel:*
- 1/2 cup golden brown sugar
- 1/3 cup chopped toasted pecans
- 1/4 cup all-purpose flour
- 2 Tablespoons unsalted melted butter

*Raspberry Fruit Sauce:*
- 3 cups fresh raspberries
- 1/3 cup + powdered sugar
- 1/4 teaspoon lemon juice

1 large mixing bowl
6 1-cup ramekins
1 large baking sheet

Baking Temperature: 375°
Baking Time: 10 minutes for crisps
20 minutes for streusel

Preheat oven to 375°. Mix all crisps ingredients in a large mixing bowl and stir to combine. Divide mixture evenly between ramekins. Place the ramekins on a large baking sheet and bake for 10 minutes. While the ramekins are baking, mix streusel ingredients in a large mixing bowl. Remove ramekins from oven and sprinkle streusel over the crisps. Continue baking the ramekins for 20 minutes or until mixture is bubbly and streusel is golden brown.

*Fruit Sauce:*

Clean raspberries as needed and puree in a food processor until completely smooth. Start adding powdered sugar a little at a time, making sure any lumps get dissolved. Add sugar until the sauce reaches your desired sweetness and consistency. If you prefer to have no seeds, strain through a fine-mesh sieve.

Drizzle fruit sauce over rhubarb crisps and serve warm. You can also serve a dish of Babcock vanilla ice cream on the side with a little fruit sauce.

**Nutritional Value Per Serving:**

| | | | |
|---|---|---|---|
| 255 Calories | 6.5 g Fat (3 g Saturated) | 3 g Protein | 50 g Carbohydrate |
| 7 g Fiber | 11 mg Sodium | 10 mg Cholesterol | |

# Franklin Street Inn
# Bed & Breakfast

**318 East Franklin Street
Appleton, WI 54911
(920)993-1711
www.franklinstreetinn.com
info@franklinstreetinn.com**

*Host: Judy Halma*

*E*xperience why the award-winning Victorian Franklin Street Inn is considered Appleton's premier Bed & Breakfast. Ideal for your next vacation, business, travel, wedding/anniversary or weekend get-away. Gracious hosts care about your comforts and ensure you will have a wonderful experience. Our 1898 Queen Anne Victorian was featured in Appleton's Historic Neighborhood City Park Home Tour. The Inn is only steps from fine restaurants, shopping, Fox Cities Performing Arts Center and Lawrence University. Enjoy the elegance of the 19th century with amenities of the 21st!

*Rates at Franklin Street Inn range from $99 to $299.
Rates include a full breakfast.*

# Farmhouse Bacon

*Our guests rave about the tantalizing aroma clear to the third floor of the inn! After eating this bacon with a new twist, you'll be adding this to your top 10 list!*

Serves 8

|  |  |
|---|---|
| 3/4 | **cup flour** |
| 3/8 | **cup brown sugar** |
| 1-1/2 | **teaspoons pepper** |
| 1-1/2 | **pounds thickly sliced bacon** |

**9" x 13" pan**
**1-1/2 quart bowl**
**kitchen shears**

**Baking Time: 10-15 minutes**
**Baking Temperature: 400°**

Preheat oven to 400°. Mix flour, brown sugar and pepper together. Sprinkle mixture on bacon strips. Place bacon in pan. Bake for 10-15 minutes or until browned and crisp.

Remove from oven and use a kitchen shears to cut strips in half for presentation serving.

***Nutritional Value Per Serving:***

| 457 Calories | 37 g Fat (12 g Saturated) | 11 g Protein | 20 g Carbohydrate |
|---|---|---|---|
| 0.5 g Fiber | 686 mg Sodium | 56 mg Cholesterol | |

# Second Wind Country Inn Bed & Breakfast

**30475 Carlson Road**
**Ashland, WI 54806**
**(715)682-1000**
**www.secondwindcountryinn.com**

*Hosts: Mark & Kelly Illick*

ome catch your breath at Second Wind Country Inn. Our name reflects what we want our guests to experience. This welcoming country Inn is located in Northern Wisconsin in the rural Ashland area. We have 3 suites: "Northern Lights Loft" which is great for small gatherings of friends and family (up to 10 persons), "Cranberry Cove" and "The Bear Den." Each room has a private bath and whirlpool. Our guests enjoy our northwoods/lodge atmosphere with 35 acres to ramble, a campfire ring, timber framed decks and our gathering room.

*Rates at Second Wind Country Inn range from $99 to $159.*
*Rates include a full breakfast.*

# Second Wind Breakfast Casserole

*This breakfast casserole is so easy and so good! I've been making it for years and still it's my children's favorite. Now that we've opened Second Wind, it's my most requested recipe.*

Serves 8-10

3  **cups herb croutons**
1  **package (12 ounces) breakfast sausage, browned and crumbled**
2  **cups shredded Cheddar cheese**
6  **eggs, beaten**
3  **cups milk, divided**
1  **can (10.75 ounces) cream of mushroom soup**

1 **large mixing bowl**
**9" x 13" glass baking pan frying pan**

**Baking Time: 1-1/2 hours**
**Baking Temperature: 325°**

Grease baking dish. Place croutons on bottom. Layer browned sausage crumbles. Layer cheese. Beat eggs in large mixing bowl. Add 2-1/2 cups milk to egg mixture. Pour over ingredients layered in pan. Mix 1/2 cup milk and cream of mushroom soup. Pour over crouton, sausage, cheese, egg and milk layers. Refrigerate overnight.

Preheat oven to 325°. Bake covered for 1-1/2 hours. Uncover to brown for final 10 minutes.

### Time saving idea:

Make 2 and freeze one. I put a frozen one in the convection oven on time bake and wake up to breakfast done at 7 a.m.!

**Nutritional Value Per Serving:**

| | | | |
|---|---|---|---|
| 443 Calories | 30 g Fat (14 g Saturated) | 25 g Protein | 18 g Carbohydrate |
| 1 g Fiber | 999 mg Sodium | 228 mg Cholesterol | |

# New Yardley Inn

**3360 County E**
**Baileys Harbor, WI 54202**
**(920)839-9487**
**(888)492-7358**
**www.newyardleyinn.com**
**Yardley@dcwis.com**

*Hosts: Suzanne & Dillon Crager*

Situated on 10 wooded acres, we offer a quiet retreat at the center of the Door Peninsula. Enjoy our spacious rooms with fireplaces and whirlpools, warm hospitality and beautiful views.

*Rates at New Yardley Inn range from $85 to $175.*
*Rates include a full breakfast.*

# Sausage-Stuffed Mushrooms

*This is a delicious side dish for many meatless egg dishes. If you use smaller mushrooms, it makes a nice canapé.*

Serves 6

| | |
|---|---|
| 12 | large mushrooms |
| 2 | Tablespoons butter, divided |
| 1/2 | pound sausage, loose or casings removed |
| 1/4 | cup chopped onion |
| 1/4 | cup Parmesan cheese |
| | salt & pepper to taste |

sauté or fry pan
8" x 8" or larger baking pan

**Baking Time: 5 minutes**
**Baking Temperature: Broil**

Remove stems from mushroom caps, set caps aside, and chop stems fine. Melt 1 Tablespoon butter in sauté pan. Add chopped mushroom stems, sausage and onions. Sauté until meat is thoroughly browned and onions are soft. Drain grease. Melt remaining butter and brush on mushroom caps. Fill caps with meat mixture, top with salt and pepper, and Parmesan cheese. Place in greased pan and broil for 5 minutes. Serve hot.

*Nutritional Value Per Serving:*

| | | | |
|---|---|---|---|
| 193 Calories | 16 g Fat (6 g Saturated) | 10 g Protein | 2 g Carbohydrate |
| 1 g Fiber | 376 mg Sodium | 46 mg Cholesterol | |

# Pinehaven
# Bed & Breakfast

**E13083 Highway 33**
**Baraboo, WI 53913**
**(608)356-3489**
**www.pinehavenbnb.com**

*Hosts: Lyle & Marge Getschman*

Enjoy our quiet, scenic country setting, small lake, gazebo and gardens. Four rooms are attractively decorated, some with wicker, antiques and country décor. A cottage is available with a whirlpool. You can walk along the Baraboo River or visit the area's many fine restaurants and attractions.

*Rates at Pinehaven Bed & Breakfast range from $99 to $145.*
*Rates include a full breakfast.*

# Fresh Fruit Coffee Cake

*This coffee cake can be a great patriotic treat if you choose blueberries and raspberries as your fresh fruit.*

Serves 9-12

*Cake:*
- 1 package (8 ounces) cream cheese, softened
- 1/2 cup (1 stick) butter, softened
- 3/4 cup sugar
- 1/4 cup milk
- 2 eggs, beaten
- 1 teaspoon vanilla
- 2 cups flour
- 1 teaspoon baking powder
- 1/2 teaspoon baking soda
- 1/4 teaspoon salt

*Filling:*
- 3 cups sliced fruit or berries

*Topping:*
- 1/3 cup brown sugar
- 1/2 cup nuts , chopped

1 medium mixing bowl
9" x 13" baking pan
Baking Time: 40 minutes
Baking Temperature: 350°

Preheat oven to 350°. Beat the cream cheese and butter together until fluffy. Add sugar, milk, eggs and vanilla. Stir in the dry ingredients. Spread half of the batter into a greased baking pan. Spread the filling over the batter. Dot remaining batter over filling. Sprinkle the topping evenly. Bake for 40 minutes.

*Nutritional Value Per Serving:*
466 Calories   25 g Fat (12 g Saturated)  8 g Protein   55 g Carbohydrate
2 g Fiber   359 mg Sodium   102 mg Cholesterol

# Old Rittenhouse Inn

**301 Rittenhouse Avenue**
**P.O. Box 584**
**Bayfield, WI 54814**
**(715)779-5111**
**(800)779-2129**
**www.rittenhouseinn.com**
**gourmet@rittenhouseinn.com**

*Host: Larry Cicero*

*T*he history of this Inn begins in 1890 when the rambling Queen Anne-style home with wraparound veranda, dormer windows and massive gables was completed as a summer home for Civil War General Allen C. Fuller. Today, the Inn is home to 24 luxurious guest rooms and a full service restaurant. The Inn has been featured in Bon Appetit, Midwest Living and Gourmet magazines for its impeccable service and gourmet cuisine. Open all year, the Inn is a popular destination for weddings, receptions, romantic getaways, family reunions and small business retreats.

*Rates at Old Rittenhouse Inn range from $99 to $299.*
*Rates include a continental plus breakfast.*

# Smoked Trout Salad with almond toast

*Created by Innkeeper Mary Phillips, this quick, easy and delicious dish has been a favorite salad of our restaurant guests for over 20 years. We're certain that your guests will love it, too!*

Serves 6-8

*Dressing:*
- 1/2 cup lemon juice
- 1/4 cup orange juice concentrate
- 1 Tablespoon white wine vinegar
- 1 Tablespoon Dijon-style mustard
- 3/4 cup mayonnaise
- 1-1/2 Tablespoons minced shallots
- 2 Tablespoons chopped cilantro
- 1 cup diced tomatoes
- salt & pepper to taste

*Salad:*
- 2 cups fresh spinach, broken
- 2 cups red lettuce, broken
- 2 cups romaine lettuce, broken
- 18 ounces smoked trout, flaked
- 1 cup slivered almonds

food processor (for dressing and almond toast)
1 medium saucepan
9" x 12" baking pan
chilled salad plates for serving

*Dressing:*

Blend first five ingredients in food processor. Salt and pepper to taste. Place in medium saucepan. Stir in the shallots, cilantro and tomatoes. Heat just to boiling point. Remove from heat.

*Salad:*

Toss the greens together and place on chilled plates. Place flaked trout on greens. Sprinkle with almonds. Drizzle with dressing. Garnish with a fresh, edible flower. Serve with almond toast.

*Almond Toast:*
- 3 ounces butter, softened
- 1 Tablespoon finely chopped fresh basil
- 1 cup slivered almonds
- 12 slices French bread, sliced 1-1/2 inches thick on a bias

Process butter, basil, and almonds in a food processor until the mixture is creamy. Coat the bread slices on each side with almond butter. Wrap in foil and heat in 350° oven for 10-15 minutes. Open foil and brown for 5 minutes. Keep warm.

*Nutritional Value Per Serving:*

835 Calories    53 g Fat (11 g Saturated)   37 g Protein     58 g Carbohydrate

9 g Fiber    774 mg Sodium    97 mg Cholesterol

# Cameo Rose
# Victorian Country
# Inn

**1090 Severson Road**
**Belleville, WI 53508**
**(608)424-6340**
**(866)424-6340**
**www.cameorose.com**
**innkeeper@cameorose.com**

*Hosts: Dawn & Gary Bahr*

Nestled amidst 120 acres of rolling hills and scenic woodland, Cameo Rose provides a luxuriously comfortable stay. We invite you to enjoy over four miles of trimmed trails, acres of gardens featuring lovely gazebos and pergolas with swings and hammocks, and excellent birding and wildlife viewing. So close to Madison, several charming tourist communities, fine dining and first class shopping; so far from the stress you left behind. Romantic, peaceful and relaxing. Welcome!

*Rates at Cameo Rose range from $129 to $219.*
*Rates include a full breakfast.*

# Cameo Rose Crustless Quiche

*We take pride in providing a very memorable breakfast and this is one of our most requested entrée recipes! Local cheeses and farm fresh ingredients make this quiche unique and delicious. It is simple to prepare and you can substitute frozen spinach for the fresh, any cheese that you like and any sausage that you prefer. We serve it with homemade bread and a variety of Amish jams as our entrée course, after fresh roasted coffee, specialty juices, fruit and sweetbread courses.*

Makes 4-6 slices

6 links precooked Jones Golden Brown Light Sausages, chopped

1/4 cup finely diced sweet red pepper

1 cup cooked spinach (can use frozen, well drained)

1 cup shredded Baby Swiss cheese

1/2 cup shredded Asiago cheese

1/4 cup shredded Pepper Jack cheese

1/4 cup shredded Cheddar cheese

1 cup heavy whipping cream

6 extra large eggs

1/4 teaspoon Mrs. Dash with garlic

paprika and parsley to garnish, as desired

salt and pepper to taste

9" glass deep dish pie plate
1 medium mixing bowl (to hold eggs and cream)

Baking Time: 15 minutes uncovered, 30 minutes covered
Baking Temperature: 425° uncovered, 325° covered

Preheat oven to 425°. Spray pie plate with nonstick cooking spray; coat all sides and bottom. Chop sausage links into small pieces and put in pie plate bottom. Add the following ingredients in order: diced red pepper, drained spinach and all cheeses except Cheddar.

Place eggs in medium mixing bowl and beat slightly. Add heavy cream and Mrs. Dash; blend with eggs. Pour cream and egg mixture over cheese in pie plate. Stir with a fork to mix all ingredients. Top with Cheddar cheese and bake as directed. Bake uncovered for 15 minutes at 425°, then reduce temperature of oven to 325° and bake for an additional 30 minutes covered.

Allow to set for 5-10 minutes after baking. Cut into 4-6 slices. Garnish on plates with parsley and paprika.

***Nutritional Value Per Serving:***

| | | | |
|---|---|---|---|
| 464 Calories | 35 g Fat (18 g Saturated) | 32 g Protein | 7 g Carbohydrate |
| 2 g Fiber | 1086 mg Sodium | 458 mg Cholesterol | |

# The Cream Pitcher
# Bed & Breakfast

**16334 Gault Hollow Road**
**Blue River, WI 53518**
**(608)536-3607**
**(866)391-2900**
**www.mwt.net/~crmptchr**
**crmptchr@mwt.net**

*Hosts: Diane & Vern Dalberg*

The Cream Pitcher Bed & Breakfast is built on our historic farm, established in 1854. Situated among the hills in Richland County, this unglaciated area offers awesome beauty as well as outdoor activities in every season. There are more than 3 miles of hiking trails through the 100 acres of woodlands. Watch deer, turkeys and other wildlife; see and hear many species of birds. Enjoy the creek that flows close by. Enjoy hiking, biking, snowshoeing, fishing or just relaxing. Our rooms have private baths, queen size beds, and each has its own entrance. One room has a whirlpool bath for two; the other has its own screen porch.

*Rates at The Cream Pitcher are $80.*
*Rates include a full breakfast.*

# Mexicana Brunch Pie

*Easy to prepare, Mexicana Brunch Pie has a wonderful, smooth texture and just the right amount of "bite." I serve this dish with lightly fried potatoes with a little chopped, fresh chives and jalapeno brats.*

Serves 6

5   eggs, beaten
2   Tablespoons butter, melted
1/4 cup flour
1/2 teaspoon baking powder
1   carton (8 ounces) cream style cottage cheese
2   cups shredded Monterey Jack cheese
1   can (4 ounces) chopped green chiles, drained

**electric mixer with large mixing bowl**
**9" pie plate**

**Baking Time: 30 minutes**
**Baking Temperature: 400° then 350°**

Preheat oven to 400°. Combine the first 4 ingredients in mixing bowl. Beat well at medium speed with electric mixer. Stir in remaining ingredients; pour into a well-buttered pie plate.

Bake uncovered at 400° for 10 minutes, and then reduce the heat to 350°. Bake at this temperature for about 20 minutes or until set. Let cool several minutes before cutting into wedges to serve.

**Nutritional Value Per Serving:**

| | | | |
|---|---|---|---|
| 321 Calories | 23 g Fat (13 g Saturated) | 21 g Protein | 7 g Carbohydrate |
| 0.5 g Fiber | 590 mg Sodium | 231 mg Cholesterol | |

# The Hillcrest Inn & Carriage House

**540 Storle Avenue**
**Burlington, WI 53105**
**(262)763-4706**
**(800)313-9030**
**www.thehillcrestinn.com**
**hillcrest@thehillcrestinn.com**

*Hosts: Gayle & Mike Hohner*

Tranquility awaits you at this 1908 Edwardian estate. Set on four lofty acres, the property offers panoramic views of waterways and multiple flower gardens. The stately Main House has been meticulously restored to its original splendor, and the Carriage House offers additional luxurious rooms. A formal four-course breakfast is served on fine china and stemware each morning.

*Rates at The Hillcrest Inn range from $100 to $200.*
*Rates include a full breakfast.*

# Chocolate Orange Tart

*Since Burlington is known as "Chocolate City," we serve chocolate in every breakfast – often as a decadent dessert.*

Serves 12

**Tart:**
- 1-1/2 cups flour
- 1/2 cup powdered sugar
- 1/2 teaspoon salt
- 1/2 cup butter
- 2/3 cup pecan pieces, chopped

**Filling:**
- 1 jar (16 ounces) orange marmalade

**Topping:**
- 2 cups chocolate chips
- 1/2 cup half-and-half

12" spring form pan
1 small mixing bowl
1 medium mixing bowl

Baking Time: 10 minutes
Baking Temperature: 350°

**Tart:**
Preheat oven to 350°. Combine flour, sugar, salt and butter in a medium mixing bowl. Microwave for 1 minute to melt the butter. Stir ingredients with a fork until combined. Press mixture into spring form pan. Scatter pecan pieces and gently push them into the crust. Bake for 10 minutes. Cool.

Spread marmalade over the crust.

**Topping:**
Combine chocolate chips and half-and-half in small mixing bowl. Microwave for 1 minute, then stir until mixture is smooth. Spread over the filling. Cool.

Serve with a twist of orange.

**Nutritional Value Per Serving:**

| | | | |
|---|---|---|---|
| 406 Calories | 22 g Fat (10 g Saturated) | 4 g Protein | 56 g Carbohydrate |
| 3 g Fiber | 180 mg Sodium | 24 mg Cholesterol | |

# McGilvray's
# Victorian
# Bed & Breakfast

**312 West Columbia Street**
**Chippewa Falls, WI 54729**
**(715)720-1600**
**(888)324-1893**
**www.mcgilvraysbb.com**
**melanie@mcgilvraysbb.com**

*Host: Melanie J Berg*

Built in 1892 by Angus J. McGilvray and his wife, Mary Lillian, this 100+-year-old home is beautifully restored and furnished with lovely antiques typical of the era. McGilvray's is located near the heart of Chippewa Falls in a quiet west hill neighborhood filled with historic homes.

Experience the Midwest in this friendly, historic city. Warm hospitality and a scrumptious breakfast are top priorities in this beautifully restored Bed & Breakfast. Relax by the fireplace on a chilly evening or enjoy one of the four porches on a summer day.

*Rates at McGilvray's Victorian Bed & Breakfast range from $79 to $110. Rates include a full breakfast.*

# Orange Currant Scones

*These light and airy scones will melt in your mouth!*

Makes 18 scones

| | |
|---|---|
| 3 | cups flour |
| 1/3 | cup white sugar |
| 2-1/2 | teaspoons baking powder |
| 1/2 | teaspoon baking soda |
| 3/4 | teaspoon salt |
| 12 | Tablespoons butter |
| 1 | cup buttermilk |
| 3/4 | cup currants |

zest of 2 oranges

**1 large mixing bowl**
**cookie sheet**
**biscuit cutter**

**Baking Time: 12 minutes**
**Baking Temperature: 400°**

Preheat oven to 400°. Mix dry ingredients (first 5 ingredients) in large mixing bowl. Cut butter into dry ingredients until it resembles coarse oatmeal. Add buttermilk and mix well. Add currants and orange zest. Form dough into a ball and roll out on a floured board until about 1/2" thick. Cut with biscuit cutter and place on an ungreased cookie sheet. Squeeze juice from oranges on top of scone and sprinkle with sugar. Bake for 12 minutes.

*Nutritional Value Per Serving:*

| 182 Calories | 8 g Fat (4 g Saturated) | 3 g Protein | 25 g Carbohydrate |
|---|---|---|---|
| 1 g Fiber | 269 mg Sodium | 21 mg Cholesterol | |

# Courthouse Square
# Bed & Breakfast

**210 East Polk Street**
**Crandon, WI 54520**
**(715)478-2549**
**(888)235-1665**
**www.courthousesquarebb.com**
**chousebb@charter.net**

*Hosts: Les & Bess Aho*

 avor gourmet breakfasts in a 'year round' garden. A panoramic watercolor mural envelops you with topiaries, cottage garden flowers and a wonderful rose arbor. Miles of Nicolet National Forest resources and out-of-the-way supper clubs add to the bucolic charm of Forest County. With no traffic lights or fast food restaurants, it's truly a place where time stops.

*Rates at Courthouse Square range from $65 to $75.*
*Rates include a full breakfast.*

# Breakfast Apple Dumplings

*A wonderful autumn and winter entrée. The tantalizing aroma will make guests think they're having apple pie for breakfast!*

Serves 8-12

**Dumplings:**
- 2 cups water
- 2 cups granulated sugar
- 1/4 cup butter or margarine
- 1/4 teaspoon cinnamon
- 1/4 teaspoon nutmeg
- 2 cups flour
- 2 teaspoons baking powder
- 1/2 teaspoon salt
- 3/4 cup shortening
- 2/3 cup milk

**Topping:**
- 1/4 cup granulated sugar
- 1/2 teaspoon cinnamon
- 3 cups shredded apples (3-4 medium)

1 large saucepan
food processor
1 large mixing bowl
1-9" x 13" pan or individual au gratin dishes

**Baking Time: 50 minutes**
**Baking Temperature: 350°**

Preheat oven to 350°. In large saucepan, combine sugar, water, margarine, cinnamon and nutmeg. Bring to a boil for 5 minutes, then set aside.

In food processor, combine flour, baking powder, and salt; cut in shortening until crumbs form. Put into large mixing bowl and add milk until moistened. Knead for 10-12 strokes. Roll out onto well-floured board to form a 12" x 10" rectangle.

Prepare topping by combining cinnamon and sugar. Sprinkle apples over dough, then sprinkle cinnamon and sugar mixture over apples.

Roll the dough, starting at the long side. Pinch to seal. Place in greased pan in 8-12 pieces or place one piece into each greased au gratin dish. Pour sauce over dumplings.

Bake at 350° for 50 minutes. Serve warm.

**Nutritional Value Per Serving:**

| | | | |
|---|---|---|---|
| 588 Calories | 26 g Fat (12 g Saturated) | 4 g Protein | 88 g Carbohydrate |
| 2 g Fiber | 320 mg Sodium | 17 mg Cholesterol | |

# Inn at Pinewood

**1820 Silver Forest Lane**
**Eagle River, WI 54521**
**(715)477-2377**
**www.inn-at-pinewood.com**
**pinewood@nnex.net**

*Hosts: Bill & Jane Weber*

As a four seasons bed & breakfast, the Inn at Pinewood offers many unique extras. The setting for the Inn is peaceful and private, and guests feel at home as soon as they enter. The massive stone fireplace offers warmth and cheer and a great place for conversation or just relaxing. For recreation, we offer boat, canoe and kayak rentals.

The original log building was built in 1934 and was used as a hunting and fishing lodge. The original charm of the lodge has been retained while additions were added. Eight cozy guestrooms have private baths, king-size beds, and balconies overlooking the lake or woods. Some rooms have double whirlpools and fireplaces. The Inn is also filled with many antiques.

Fall asleep to the sound of the loons and wake to the aroma of freshly baked muffins. Breakfasts are memorable. Guests are served in the garden dining room with large windows overlooking the woods. Watch the wildlife while enjoying a full scrumptious breakfast.

*Rates at Inn at Pinewood range from $104 to $154.*
*Rates include a full breakfast.*

# Pumpkin Nut Muffins

*The smell of these muffins baking reminds me of when I was a child and Mom would be baking on a crisp autumn day. The smell lingered in the air! But don't save these for fall baking; they are good any time of the year.*

Makes 12 muffins

**Muffins:**
- 1-3/4  cups all-purpose flour
- 1/2  cup granulated sugar
- 1  teaspoon baking powder
- 1/2  teaspoon baking soda
- 1/2  teaspoon salt
- 1/2  teaspoon ground cinnamon
- 1/2  teaspoon ground allspice
- 1/2  teaspoon ground nutmeg
- 1-1/4  cups solid pack pumpkin
- 1/2  cup buttermilk or plain yogurt
- 1  large egg, lightly beaten
- 3  Tablespoons melted butter or margarine
- 2/3 to 3/4 cup chopped walnuts

**Topping:**
- 1/4  cup brown sugar
- 1/2  teaspoon cinnamon

1 small mixing bowl
1 medium mixing bowl
12-cup muffin tin

**Baking Temperature: 375°**
**Baking Time: 25-30 minutes**

Preheat oven to 375°. Grease a 12-cup muffin tin or line with paper baking cups. In a small mixing bowl, stir together flour, sugar, baking powder, baking soda, salt, cinnamon, allspice and nutmeg. In a medium mixing bowl, combine pumpkin, buttermilk or yogurt, egg, butter or margarine, and chopped walnuts. Whisk together.

Add flour mixture to wet ingredients and stir until ingredients are moistened. (Do not over mix; a few lumps are OK). Spoon mixture into prepared muffin tin and fill cups 2/3 – 3/4 full.

Combine brown sugar and cinnamon for topping. Sprinkle topping evenly on top of batter. Bake for 25-30 minutes or until muffins are golden brown around the edges. Cool for 5 minutes and remove from pan. Serve warm.

**Nutritional Value Per Serving:**

| | | | |
|---|---|---|---|
| 205 Calories | 8 g Fat (2 g Saturated | 4 g Protein | 31 g Carbohydrate |
| 2 g Fiber | 251 mg Sodium | 26 mg Cholesterol | |

# Eagle Harbor Inn

**9914 Water Street**
**P.O. Box 588**
**Ephraim, WI 54211**
**(920)854-2121**
**(800)324-5427**
**www.eagleharbor.com**
**nedd@eagleharbor.com**

*Hosts: Nedd & Natalie Neddersen*

*O*ur graciously appointed nine room Inn, all with private baths, some with whirlpools and fireplaces, offers a main street location with pool and professional fitness room in Ephraim's Historic District. Walk to Ephraim's white sand beach, wonderful shops and intriguing galleries. We have very popular honeymoon and winter magic packages!

Our guests are given the opportunity to feel at home, whether it's the need for our strongly brewed coffee early in the morning or a dietary need for low cholesterol or no salt foods. Chef Nedd is pleased to accommodate our guests. We offer a full spread of homemade cherry granola and cereals, cherry cider and juices, and fresh seasonal fruits artfully arrayed with fresh flowers and greens, all before the entrée begins. All of our dishes are creatively garnished with fresh herbs from our kitchen garden. We are known for our breakfasts!

*Rates at Eagle Harbor Inn range from $96 to $189.*
*Rates include a full breakfast (continental plus on winter weekdays)*

# Cherry Cream Cheese Stuffed French Toast

*This entrée is our most popular because French Toast is always a favorite, and the added sweet richness of the Door County cherry cheese filling puts it 'over the top.' It is extremely easy, yet tastes like a million dollars!*

Serves 8 (2 pieces each)

*Toast:*
- 1   loaf sour dough bread
- 3   eggs
- 1/2   cup half-and-half cream
- 1/4   teaspoon nutmeg
- 1/4   teaspoon salt
- 1/4   teaspoon vanilla

*Filling:*
- 8   ounces cream cheese at room temperature
- 1/2   cup powdered sugar
- 2   Tablespoons vanilla
- 4   cups drained tart cherries

1 medium mixing bowl
1 large mixing bowl
1 large skillet

*Filling:*

In medium mixing bowl, cream together cream cheese, powdered sugar and vanilla. Add cherries and mix well.

*Toast:*

In large mixing bowl, beat together eggs, cream, nutmeg, salt and vanilla until blended. Thickly slice sour dough bread. Slice each piece 3/4 way through bread to make a slit pocket. Stuff each piece with cherry cheese filling (above). Dip in egg batter. Fry in skillet until both sides are a golden brown. Sprinkle with powdered sugar and serve immediately.

***Nutritional Value Per Serving:***

| | | | |
|---|---|---|---|
| 382 Calories | 14 g Fat (7 g Saturated) | 12 g Protein | 50 g Carbohydrate |
| 3.5 g Fiber | 640 mg Sodium | 111 mg Cholesterol | |

# French Country Inn
# of Ephraim

**3052 Spruce Lane**
**P.O. Box 129**
**Ephraim, WI 54211**
**(920)854-4001**
**frenchcountryinn@dcwis.com**

*Hosts: Walt Fisher & Joan Fitzpatrick*

The house, built in 1911 as a summer home, complements Door County's natural environment. Our breakfast, focusing on organic and local products, complements today's healthful lifestyle.

*Rates at French Country Inn of Ephraim range from $67 to $95.*
*Rates include a Continental Plus breakfast.*

# French Egg Puffs

*This is an easy to make egg dish, but what a show! Put them in the oven to bake as you serve a first course of fruit and sweet bread (scone, muffin, etc.) plus coffee or tea. This second course dish needs to be served immediately because they will sink as they cool.*

Serves 6

6 eggs (preferably free range)
1 cup 1% milk
1 cup all-purpose flour
(preferably organic)
1/3 cup sugar
1/2 teaspoon salt
6 Tablespoons finely chopped
herbs from the garden
(parsley, thyme, oregano,
chives, etc.) or 3 Tablespoons
dried herbs of Provance
2 Tablespoons butter

*Toppings:*
Chopped tomatoes
Sour cream

1 large mixing bowl
1 baking tray
1 whisk
6-6" ovenproof ramekins

Baking Temperature: 400°
Baking Time: 20 minutes

Preheat oven to 400°. Whisk eggs, milk, flour, sugar and salt together in large mixing bowl. Add fresh or dried herbs to mixture. Butter each ramekin, place on baking tray and warm in oven to 5 minutes. Pour mixture into warmed ramekins and bake for 20 minutes or until golden and puffed.

Serve immediately by placing each ramekin on an individual serving plate and sprinkling with chopped tomatoes and sour cream.

*Nutritional Value Per Serving:*

| | | | |
|---|---|---|---|
| 270 Calories | 12 g Fat (5 g Saturated) | 11 g Protein | 30 g Carbohydrate |
| 1 g Fiber | 327 mg Sodium | 261 mg Cholesterol | |

Fall River, WI

# Fountain Prairie Inn & Farms

W1901 Highway 16
Fall River, WI 53932
(920)484-3618
(866)883-4775
www.fountainprairie.com
priske@centurytel.net

*Hosts: Dorothy & John Priske*

*L*et us pamper you with a sumptuous breakfast to start your day and give you energy for the activities ahead—browsing the quaint shops in Columbus, walking the trails through tall grass prairie and wetlands on our farm, or just relaxing. Our large front porch, deck and gazebo invite you to unwind in the summer or seek out a cozy sitting room any time of year.

*Rates at Fountain Prairie Inn & Farms range from $70 to $150.*
*Rates include a full breakfast.*

# Spinach Frittata

*We try to use locally produced ingredients whenever possible. The ingredients for this simple frittata can easily be found at local farmers' markets. Having our own herb garden allows us to use the freshest seasonings possible and gives our recipes that extra zing!*

Serves 4-6

1 teaspoon butter
1 cup fresh spinach leaves
8 eggs
1/2 cup half-and-half
1/2 teaspoon salt
1/4 teaspoon pepper
1 Tablespoon chopped fresh basil leaves
3/4 cup grated Swiss cheese
1 medium tomato, thinly sliced

8 x 8-inch glass baking pan
1 medium mixing bowl

Baking Temperature: 325°
Baking Time: 20-25 minutes

Preheat oven to 325°. Generously butter baking pan. In medium mixing bowl, combine eggs, half-and-half, salt, pepper and basil. Whisk until well blended. Stir in Swiss cheese. Pour into baking dish. Arrange tomato slices on top. Bake for 20-25 minutes, until center is almost set. Let frittata rest for 5-10 minutes before serving.

*Nutritional Value Per Serving:*

| | | | |
|---|---|---|---|
| 272 Calories | 18 g Fat (8 g Saturated) | 20 g Protein | 6 g Carbohydrate |
| 0.5 g Fiber | 535 mg Sodium | 450 mg Cholesterol | |

# Lakeside Bed & Breakfast

**Fisher Lake**
**Box 54**
**Florence, WI 54121**
**(715)528-3259**

*Hosts: Ron & Rita McMullen*

ooking to get away from it all? Look no further than Lakeside Bed & Breakfast. While geographically located in northeastern Wisconsin, Lakeside exists in a state all of its own. On the shore of beautiful Fisher Lake and Gateway to the Nicolet National Forest, Lakeside's peace and tranquility would make Thoreau envious.

In the morning, there's breakfast served by candlelight. It's a meal that's designed to make your day before it even gets started. Lakeside Bed & Breakfast has been featured in *Midwest Living*.

*Rates at Lakeside Bed & Breakfast are $85.*
*Rates include a full breakfast.*

# Cinnamon Carrot Cake with cream cheese frosting

*This quick and easy recipe is also low fat! Serve an old-time favorite without all of the fat of traditional recipe!*

Serves 12

*Cake:*
- 2-1/2 cups unbleached flour
- 1-1/4 cups brown sugar
- 2 teaspoons baking soda
- 2 teaspoons ground cinnamon
- 3/4 cup plus 2 Tablespoons apple juice
- 4 egg whites
- 2 teaspoons vanilla extract
- 3 cups grated carrots (about 6 medium carrots)
- 1/3 cup dark raisins

*Frosting:*
- 8 ounces non-fat cream cheese
- 1 cup non-fat ricotta cheese
- 1/2 cup powdered sugar
- 1 teaspoon vanilla extract

1 medium mixing bowl
9" x 13" cake pan

Baking Time: 30-35 minutes
Baking Temperature: 350°

*Cake:*

Preheat oven to 350°. Combine flour, brown sugar, baking soda and cinnamon; stir to mix well. Add juice, egg whites and vanilla extract; mix well. Stir in the carrots and raisins. Spray cake pan with nonstick cooking spray and spread batter evenly in pan. Bake for 30-35 minutes.

*Frosting:*

Mix all ingredients together and spread on cool cake.

*Nutritional Value Per Serving:*

| | | | |
|---|---|---|---|
| 272 Calories | 20 g Fat (2 g Saturated) | 9 g Protein | 54 g Carbohydrate |
| 2 g Fiber | 388 mg Sodium | 8 mg Cholesterol | |

# La Grange
# Bed & Breakfast

**1050 East Street**
**Fort Atkinson, WI 53538**
**(920)563-1421**
**www.1928barn.com**
**lagrange@compufort.com**

*Hosts: Dennis & Gerry Rybicke*

*R*elax in the cozy atmosphere of a 1928 remodeled barn. Enjoy the privacy of the enclosed deck as you feel the soft spray of the water fountain. Then enjoy the wonderful entertainment and food at the nearby Fireside Dinner Theatre or the special atmosphere of Café Carpe or I Love Franky's. It's your choice to do or <u>not</u> to do at La Grange.

*Rates at La Grange Bed & Breakfast range from $75 to $89.*
*Rates include a full breakfast.*

# Moist Tofu Brownies

*Who knew that tofu could taste this delicious? These low-fat chocolate goodies melt in your mouth. Enjoy a healthful treat without giving up taste.*

Makes 30 brownies

**Brownies:**
2-1/4 cups sugar
1-1/2 cups unbleached flour
1-1/2 cups cocoa powder
1-1/2 teaspoons baking powder
1-1/2 teaspoons baking soda
1/8 teaspoon sea salt
1-1/3 cups unsweetened
applesauce
1 cup (8 ounces) low-fat tofu
3/4 cup soy milk
2 egg whites
1 teaspoon real vanilla extract
1 teaspoon almond extract
nonstick cooking spray

**Glaze:**
1 cup cocoa powder
1-1/2 cups honey
1 teaspoon real vanilla extract
1 teaspoon almond extract

1 small mixing bowl
1 large mixing bowl
food processor
9" x 13" glass baking dish

Baking Time: 40-45 minutes
Baking Temperature: 325°

**Brownies:**
Preheat oven to 325°. Sift sugar, flour, cocoa powder, baking powder, baking soda and salt into large mixing bowl. In a food processor, combine applesauce, tofu, soy milk, egg whites and flavorings until smooth. Stir tofu mixture into dry ingredients until smooth. Pour mixture into lightly sprayed baking dish. Bake for 40-45 minutes or until a toothpick inserted in center comes out clean. Cool in pan before glazing.

**Glaze:**
In a small mixing bowl, mix cocoa powder and honey until smooth. Add extracts. Pour glaze over cooled brownies. Cut into 2" x 2" pieces and serve.

**Nutritional Value Per Serving:**
169 Calories    2 g Fat (1 g Saturated)    3 g Protein    40 g Carbohydrate
3 g Fiber    103 mg Sodium    0 mg Cholesterol

# McConnell Inn

**497 South Lawson Drive**
**Green Lake, WI 54941**
**(920)294-6430**
**(888)238-8625**
**www.mcconnellinn.com**
**info@mcconnellinn.com**

*Hosts: Mary-Jo & Scott Johnson*

reen Lake has a long history of hospitality, being the oldest resort area west of Niagara Falls. We are pleased to carry on the tradition in an elegant Victorian, boasting parquet floors and leather wainscoting. We offer 5 guest rooms, each with private bath and queen or king size beds. For sumptuous relaxation, our suite features Jacuzzi, fireplace, 14-foot vaulted ceilings and sitting room with a panoramic view of the lake. We serve a hearty, full breakfast prepared by Mary-Jo, a pastry chef. Enjoy Wisconsin's deepest lake with swimming, boating and fishing, or partake in golfing, hiking, biking, antiquing and cross-country skiing.

*Rates at McConnell Inn range from $60 to $175.*
*Rates include a full breakfast.*

# Speckpfannkuchen mit apfel

*This recipe was introduced to us by our German foreign exchange student. It is now one of our Inn favorites. I converted this recipe from metric weight.*

Serves 6

*Crepe:*
- 4 eggs
- 2-1/2 cups milk
- 1 teaspoon salt
- 2 Tablespoons sugar
- 1-3/4 cups flour

*Topping:*
- 3 apples, Empire or Macintosh
- 2 Tablespoons butter
- 3 Tablespoons brown sugar
- 2 teaspoons cinnamon powdered sugar

- 1 large mixing bowl
- 1 small sauté pan
- 1 large crepe pan
- ladle

*Crepe:*

In a large mixing bowl, beat eggs well. Add milk and continue beating. Sprinkle sugar on mixture and beat. Sift flour and salt into egg mixture. Stir until well mixed. Spray crepe pan with nonstick cooking spray. Heat pan. Ladle small amount of batter into pan and tilt until bottom is covered. Flip when brown. Remove from pan and keep warm until ready to fill.

*Topping:*

Peel, core and slice apples. Melt butter in small sauté pan. Add brown sugar and cinnamon to butter. Stir in apples. Sauté over low heat until apples are warm and tender. Fill crepe with apple mix (approximately 2 Tablespoons per crepe), roll and sprinkle with powdered sugar.

May serve with maple syrup.

**Nutritional Value Per Serving:**

| | | | |
|---|---|---|---|
| 347 Calories | 10 g Fat (4 g Saturated) | 12 g Protein | 54 g Carbohydrate |
| 3 g Fiber | 514 mg Sodium | 159 mg Cholesterol | |

# The Happy Horse
# Bed & Breakfast

**24273 State Highway 27**
**Holcombe, WI 54745**
**(715)239-0707**
**www.happyhorsebb.com**
**happyhorsebb@centurytel.net**

*Hosts: Alan & Sandra Ricker*

Built in the late 1920s, the original farmstead was home to a family with 15 children! In keeping with the rural setting, The Happy Horse is a blend of modern comfort and country pleasures. Each season has a special treat for guests—watching spring-born colts in the pasture, sharing the shade on the porch with a barn cat, snuggling under handmade quilts in one of our four bedrooms. Our breakfasts are sumptuous, the farm animals friendly and the atmosphere is peaceful… come for a visit!

*Rates at The Happy Horse Bed & Breakfast are $69.*
*Rates include a full breakfast.*

# Florentine Eggs

*This recipe will make a fantastic vegetarian brunch, served with a fresh fruit salad.*

Serves 6

1 box (10 ounces) frozen spinach, thawed & squeezed dry
9 hard cooked eggs, peeled and halved lengthwise
3 Tablespoons mayonnaise
1 Tablespoon cider vinegar
2 teaspoons instant minced onion
1/2 teaspoon dry mustard
1/2 teaspoon salt
1/4 teaspoon ground red pepper (cayenne)
1 jar (16 ounces) alfredo sauce
1 cup fresh bread crumbs
2 Tablespoons melted butter

1  small mixing bowl
2-quart baking dish

Baking Time: 25-30 minutes
Baking Temperature: 350°

Preheat oven to 350°. Lightly coat a shallow baking dish with nonstick cooking spray. Scatter spinach evenly in baking dish. Remove egg yolks from eggs; mash yolks with mayonnaise, vinegar, onion, mustard, salt and red pepper until smooth. Spoon into hollow of each white. Arrange eggs yolk side down on spinach. Pour alfredo sauce over eggs to cover. Mix crumbs and butter together. Sprinkle over sauce. Bake uncovered for 25-30 minutes until sauce is nice and bubbly.

***Nutritional Value Per Serving:***
552 Calories     33 g Fat (16 g Saturated)  35 g Protein     40 g Carbohydrate
16 g Fiber        1305 mg Sodium           376 mg Cholesterol

# Honeybee Inn
# Bed & Breakfast

**611 East Walnut Street**
**Horicon, WI 53032**
**(920)485-4855**
**www.honeybeeinn.com**
**innkeeper@honeybeeinn.com**

*Hosts: Barbara & Fred Ruka*

*I*mmerse yourselves in our beautiful 100-year-old, historic Bed & Breakfast Inn, built for an heiress! Honeybee Inn Bed & Breakfast is the perfect location for that romantic getaway, birding adventure, anniversary, wedding night, reunion or business stay. Guests are constantly telling us that we are one of the finest Bed & Breakfast Inns that they have ever stayed in. Attention to detail is evident everywhere. You, too, will be spoiled with the finest amenities, including deluxe whirlpools, six fireplaces, private modern bathrooms, plush luxury towels, turn down chocolates, feather beds, TV's/VCR's/CD players, high speed internet, and our famous scrumptious breakfasts. Make any occasion truly magical by reserving a room at the Honeybee Inn in the heart of Horicon, right next to the famous Horicon Marsh Wildlife and Recreation area.

*Rates at Honeybee Inn Bed & Breakfast range from $109 to $210.*
*Rates include a full breakfast.*

*Yummy!*

# Honeybee Inn Sour Cream Coffee Cake

*Barb has been making this coffee cake for 25 years. It never fails to get great raves for its fantastic flavor and tender, moist texture.*

Serves 12

*Cake:*
- 1 cup butter
- 2 cups sugar
- 4 eggs
- 2 cups sour cream
- 4 cups flour
- 1 teaspoon baking powder
- 1 teaspoon baking soda
- 1 teaspoon salt

*Topping:*
- 1-1/2 cups sugar
- 2 teaspoons cinnamon
- 1 stick (1/2 cup) butter, melted

*Mix cinnamon and sugar together.*

2 large mixing bowls
1 small mixing bowl
mixer
9" x 13" baking dish

**Baking Time: 40 minutes**
**Baking Temperature: 350°**

Preheat oven to 350°. Mix dry ingredients in large mixing bowl. In another bowl, cream butter and sugar well. Add eggs, one at a time, beating well after each egg. Alternate adding sour cream with dry ingredient mixture. Spread half of batter in greased baking dish. Sprinkle half of topping mixture over batter. Add rest of batter by Tablespoons on topping. Smooth with knife. Sprinkle remaining topping. Pour melted butter over top evenly. Bake for 40 minutes.

*Nutritional Value Per Serving:*

| | | | |
|---|---|---|---|
| 689 Calories | 33 g Fat (17 g Saturated) | 8 g Protein | 92 g Carbohydrate |
| 1 g Fiber | 547 mg Sodium | 148 mg Cholesterol | |

# Phipps Inn
# Bed & Breakfast

**1005 Third Street**
**Hudson, WI 54016**
**(715)386-0800**
**(888)865-9388**
**www.phippsinn.com**
**info@phippsinn.com**

*Hosts: Mary Ellen & Rich Cox*

Described as the "Grand Dame" of Queen Anne houses in Hudson, the Phipps Inn is a luxurious 1884 Victorian mansion nestled in the charming setting of Hudson's historic Third Street. Step through the door and back across one hundred years into a graceful era of leaded glass windows and finely crafted furnishings. Enjoy quiet conversations in the parlor around a glowing fire or play a game of pool in the Billiards Room. A lavish breakfast, presented on gleaming china and crystals, is served either in your room or in the dining room. All of the guest rooms have fireplaces, double whirlpool tubs, private baths with shower, and queen-size beds. The Phipps Inn is an elegant, romantic retreat waiting to enchant you.

*Rates at Phipps Inn range from $129 to $209.*
*Rates include a full breakfast.*

# Sweet & Sour Grapefruit

*Start your special breakfast by giving grapefruit a new and delicious twist. It's easy, it's pretty and the combination of creamy sweet and sour flavors is surprising. The grapefruit and the sauce can be prepared separately ahead of time and warmed at the last minute. We made this for each other long before we became innkeepers and it's become a favorite first course for our guests.*

Serves 4

2  grapefruits, red preferred
4  maraschino cherries with stems
   ground nutmeg

*Sour cream sauce:*
1/4  cup sour cream
1  Tablespoon brown sugar
*Mix well.*

4  individual fruit bowls

Cut grapefruit in half, section and place in individual bowls. Warm all four halves at one time in the microwave for 1 minute. Place a Tablespoon of sour cream sauce in the middle of each grapefruit. Warm all four halves again for 30-40 seconds. Sprinkle sparingly with nutmeg. Garnish each half with a cherry.

**Nutritional Value Per Serving:**

| 105 Calories | 3 g Fat (2 g Saturated) | 1.5 g Protein | 19 g Carbohydrate |
| 2 g Fiber | 13 mg Sodium | 6 mg Cholesterol | |

# Four Gables
# Bed & Breakfast

**W5648, Highway 14-61**
**La Crosse, WI 54601**
**(608)788-7958**
**www.bedandbreakfast.com/listing.aspx?id=602305**
**forgables@juno.com**

*Hosts: Gerald & Nancy Jorgensen*

Our 1906 rural Queen Anne home is on the National Registry of Historical Places. The décor is uncluttered Victorian with antiques of distinction. Within five miles, there is skiing, antiquing, river adventures and cruising, festivals, shopping, hiking, gardens and historic downtown LaCrosse. The gourmet breakfast is enjoyed by new and repeat guests. Our goal is to make our home your home while you are visiting this area.

*Rates at Four Gables Bed & Breakfast range from $55 to $90.*
*Rates include a full breakfast.*

# Chocolate Molten Cake

*This recipe is for chocolate lovers!! Because it is frozen and then baked, there is no last minute hassle. I found this recipe in an old book. It was handwritten on a slip of paper tucked in the book. The book is long since gone, but the recipe remains a favorite.*

Makes 4 individual servings

3 ounces good quality semi-sweet chocolate, finely chopped
1 ounce unsweetened chocolate, finely chopped
6 Tablespoons plus 2 teaspoons unsalted butter, softened
6 Tablespoons sugar

2 large eggs
6 Tablespoons all-purpose flour
1/2 teaspoon baking powder
1 Tablespoon unsweetened cocoa powder
whipped cream for garnish
cocoa powder for garnish

4 – 4.5 ounce ramekins
double boiler
electric mixer

**Baking Time: 10-11 minutes**
**Baking Temperature: 375°**

Lightly butter ramekins. In top of double boiler, melt chocolates (both semi-sweet and unsweetened). Remove from heat and stir in 6 Tablespoons butter and sugar until smooth. Add eggs, flour, baking powder and cocoa. With electric mixer, beat at medium-high speed until pale and very thick, about 5 minutes. Place mixture in prepared ramekins, filling about half full. Cover with plastic wrap and freeze for at least 3 hours.

When ready to serve, preheat oven to 375°. Remove plastic wrap and place ramekins on middle shelf of oven. Bake until edges are set but centers are still shiny, about 10-11 minutes. Invert pudding cakes onto plates and serve immediately, garnished with whipped cream and a dusting of cocoa powder.

Desserts can be served directly from ramekins if desired, but presentation is more pleasing if served on a plate.

***Nutritional Value Per Serving:***

| | | | |
|---|---|---|---|
| 463 Calories | 32 g Fat (19 g Saturated) | 7 g Protein | 45 g Carbohydrate |
| 3 g Fiber | 103 mg Sodium | 157 mg Cholesterol | |

# Trillium

**E10596 East Salem Ridge Road**
**La Farge, WI 54639**
**(608)625-4492**
**www.trilliumcottage.com**
**info@trilliumcottage.com**

*Host: Rosanne Boyett*

Celebrating our 20th year! Here on our organic family farm, we offer two private guest cottages. Each is fully furnished with complete kitchen, full bath, wood burning fireplace, and porch with porch swing. Enjoy farm life in a peaceful, quiet, private setting. Families are welcome. Open year round.

*Rates at Trillium range from $65 to $110.*
*Rates include a full breakfast.*

# Oat Bran Bread

*This is a wonderfully delicious recipe that is easy to make! Although preparation time is longer, the results are worth it! It is best to begin preparation the night before to allow the mixture to ripen.*

Makes 2 medium-size loaves

| | |
|---|---|
| 3 | Tablespoons honey |
| 1-1/2 | teaspoons dry yeast |
| 1-1/2 | cups plus 2 Tablespoons oat bran |
| 2 | teaspoons salt |
| 2 | cups warm water |
| 3-1/2 to 4-1/2 | cups all-purpose flour |
| 1 | large egg white |

2 large mixing bowls
baking stone

**Baking Time: 45-50 minutes**
**Baking Temperature: 375°**

In a large bowl, stir together water, honey and yeast. Allow to sit for 10-15 minutes until yeast is dissolved and frothy. Stir in oat bran. (Do not use processed oat cereal). Once the bran has absorbed the liquid, stir in 1 cup of the flour. Cover, place in a warm spot & allow dough to ripen.

After 4-6 hours, stir down, add salt and stir. Then, 1cup at a time, stir in the flour until a nice, firm dough is formed. Turn out onto a floured surface and knead for 10-15 minutes. Place in oiled bowl, cover and place in a warm spot until the dough doubles in size (2 hours or longer). Punch dough down. Divide in half. Shape into round loaves. Place on baking stone. Cover and allow to double in size (about 1 hour).

Preheat oven to 375°. Brush the top of the loaves with egg white and sprinkle with remaining oat bran. Bake for 45-50 minutes until nicely browned and loaves sound hollow when tapped on the bottom.

Because of the long preparation time, it is best to begin the night before so that the dough has sufficient time to ripen (as described in first paragraph).

*Nutritional Value Per Serving:*

| | | | |
|---|---|---|---|
| 129 Calories | 1 g Fat (0.1 g Saturated) | 4.5 g Protein | 28 g Carbohydrate |
| 2 g Fiber | 237 mg Sodium | 0 mg Cholesterol | |

# General Boyd's
# Bed & Breakfast

**W2915 South Lakeshore Drive**
**Lake Geneva, WI 53147**
**(262)248-3543**
**www.generalboydsbb.com**
**morton4u@execpc.com**

*Hosts: Susan & Bob Morton*

Take the stately historic home of General John W. Boyd; add 5 acres and a yard full of flowers with paths to places in which you can escape, and you'll know why you chose this Bed & Breakfast. Located just 2.7 miles south of the city of Lake Geneva and 1/3 mile from the shore path, General Boyd's has been AAA rated consistently since 1997 with Three Diamonds. Come for relaxing country charm, a comfortable bed and a fabulous breakfast.

*Rates at General Boyd's range from $100 to $145.*
*Rates include a full breakfast.*

# Easy Eggs Benedict

*You can't go wrong with this recipe! It's delicious and easy! Be sure to heat eggs to the boiling point, but don't boil. This is a great recipe on asparagus or broccoli for vegetarians.*

Serves 6

| | |
|---|---|
| 1 | can (10 ounces) cream of mushroom soup (preferably Campbell's) |
| 3 | egg yolks |
| 2 | Tablespoons lemon juice |
| 3 | drops red pepper sauce |
| 1/2 | cup melted butter |
| 12 | slices Canadian bacon or ham, heated |
| 6 | English muffins |
| 12 | eggs, poached |

blender
1 small dish to melt butter
saucepan
1 large pan for poached eggs
toaster oven

**Cooking Time: 30 minutes (approx.)**

In blender, combine soup, egg yolks, lemon juice and hot pepper sauce. Cover and blend on high for a few seconds. With blender still on high speed, remove cover. Very slowly pour butter in a steady stream into the soup mixture. Blend for 3 minutes or until thick. Pour mixture into saucepan on low heat, stirring occasionally. On an oven-safe plate, toast English muffin in toaster oven. Arrange bacon or ham on buttered muffin and top with poached egg. Place muffins in toaster oven just to warm eggs and bacon or ham. Remove from oven and pour sauce over prepared muffins. Sprinkle with paprika.

***Nutritional Value Per Serving:***

| | | | |
|---|---|---|---|
| 1013 Calories | 66 g Fat (22 g Saturated) | 44 g Protein | 61 g Carbohydrate |
| 3 g Fiber | 4550 mg Sodium | 628 mg Cholesterol | |

# Victorian Treasure Inn

**115 Prairie Street**
**Lodi, WI 53555**
**(608)592-5199**
**(800)859-5199**
**www.victoriantreasure.com**
**innkeeper@victoriantreasure.com**

*Hosts: Renee & Eric Degelau*

*Victorian Treasure Inn is a AAA Four Diamond and Select Registry Inn. Named "One of the Top 10 Romantic Inns in America" by American Historic Inns.*

Victorian Treasure is a luxury, romantic Bed & Breakfast Inn featuring two 1890s Queen Anne Victorian homes located minutes from biking, hiking, wineries and Lake Wisconsin. A great romantic Inn for your wedding, honeymoon or anniversary! Most accommodations have whirlpools and fireplaces. Victorian Treasure has seven accommodations to meet your needs. Limousine service provided for your romantic ride to area restaurants and attractions.

Our five romantic deluxe suites also include a spacious two-person whirlpool bath, stereo system with cassette and CD, cable television with VCR/DVD, in-room coffeemaker, microwave and bar refrigerator. An antique mantle gas fireplace is also provided in each Hutson House suite.

Victorian Treasure Inn is found in the quaint Victorian town of Lodi, located on the National Scenic Ice Age Trail in the beautiful Wisconsin River Valley. The Inn is conveniently located in the heart of south central Wisconsin, four miles west of I-90/94, between Madison and Devil's Lake State Park and the Baraboo Hills.

*Rates at Victorian Treasure Inn range from $119 to $249.*
*Rates include a full breakfast.*

# Fruit Stuffed Pancakes

*Elegance and romance await you at Victorian Treasure Inn. Our menu combines seasonal fruits and delicious breads with large portion entrées. Featured are Wisconsin fruits, cheeses and sausage.*

Serves 6

**Pancakes:**
- 3 cups buttermilk
- 3 eggs
- 3 cups flour
- 1/4 cup plus 2 Tablespoons oil
- 1 teaspoon salt
- 3 Tablespoons sugar
- 1-1/2 teaspoons baking soda
- 1 Tablespoon baking powder

**Filling:**
- 8 ounces cream cheese, softened
- 2 Tablespoons vanilla
- 2 Tablespoons half-and-half

**Fruit Sauce:**
- 16 ounces frozen blueberries
- 2 cups water
- 1 cup sugar

1 large mixing bowl
2 medium mixing bowls
1 medium saucepan
electric griddle

Cooking Time: 20 minutes
Cooking Temperature: 325°

**Filling:**

Place cream cheese, half-and-half and vanilla in medium mixing bowl and mix at medium speed until mixed and soft. Set aside.

**Fruit Sauce:**

Place blueberries, water and sugar in medium saucepan over medium heat. Heat for 15 minutes, until blueberries start to soften. Keep warm on low heat.

**Pancakes:**

Combine dry ingredients in large mixing bowl. Beat eggs in medium mixing bowl, add buttermilk and oil, and mix well. Pour wet mixture into dry ingredients. Make medium size pancakes on griddle at 325° (makes 12 pancakes).

Place a pancake on each plate. Spread cream cheese mixture on pancake to cover 1/4" thick. Pour or ladle 1/4 cup fruit sauce on top of cream cheese. Place second pancake on top. Ladle 1/4 cup fruit sauce on top of each stack. Garnish with powdered sugar.

**Nutritional Value Per Serving:**

| | | | |
|---|---|---|---|
| 777 Calories | 32 g Fat (12 g Saturated) | 17 g Protein | 105 g Carbohydrate |
| 4 g Fiber | 1228 mg Sodium | 154 mg Cholesterol | |

# Annie's Garden
# Bed & Breakfast

**2117 Sheridan Drive**
**Madison, WI 53704**
**(608)244-2224**
**www.bbinternet.com/annies**

*Hosts: Annie & Larry Stuart*

Surrounded by trees and lush gardens, Annie's is nestled alongside a beautiful wooded vista of Warner Park on the north side of the city of Madison, with the eastern shore of Lake Mendota nearby. Miles of nature trails thread through the park. Stroll the lakeshore at sunset or explore the woods and marshes to catch glimpses of deer, fox and countless birds.

The rustic cedar shake house is a gem, owner-designed in the 1960s and full of fascinating art, antiques and collections reflecting a deep appreciation of nature. Downtown/campus is a quick 6-minute drive. Come and meet Annie, Larry and their twin Siamese catties, Firecracker and Sparkler. Please visit our website for more details about the Inn.

*Rates at Annie's Garden range from $139 to $209.*
*Rates include a full breakfast.*

# Annie's Apple Cream Pudding

*The history of this recipe goes back to 1950-1980 when there were 8 children living in our house. Those were happy, active, creative years for me, both as a designer working for the state, but especially as a mother, spending lots of time in the kitchen creating a long list of "favorites" for my family. Now, at nearly 70 years old, I still love to cook and have been doing it for 20 years at Annie's Garden Bed & Breakfast. I hope that your family will enjoy it, too. (Don't tell them, but it's very good for you!)*

Serves 8-12

| | |
|---|---|
| 4 cups skim milk | 1 cup halved fresh cranberries |
| 1/4 cup brown sugar | *(dried cranberries, whole, are OK)* |
| 1/4 cup frozen apple juice concentrate | 1-1/2 cups chopped nuts *(pecans, walnuts, almonds or combination)* |
| 1/2 teaspoon salt | 1/4 cup flaked coconut, optional |
| 2 Tablespoons powdered lemonade mix (with sugar) | |
| 2 Tablespoons soft butter | 1 large mixing bowl, microwave safe |
| 1 cup golden seedless raisins | 1 large oven-proof baking dish |
| 4 to 5 large Red Delicious apples, cored and sliced uniformly with Cuisinart. *Do not peel apples.* | (3 – 4 quarts) |
| 2-1/4 cups old-fashioned oatmeal | Baking Time: 45 minutes |
| | Baking Temperature: 350° |

Preheat oven to 350°. In a large mixing bowl, combine milk, brown sugar, apple juice, lemonade mix and butter. Heat until hot, but not boiling. Add the remaining ingredients, one at a time, in the order shown above. Mix well and put into well-buttered baking dish, making sure there is about an inch left from the rim for "bubbling." Bake for about 45 minutes or until apples are cooked but NOT mushy. I like them on the "firm side." Stir to integrate the fruit.

Serve in bowls with a dollop of sweetened sour cream and a drizzle of good caramel sauce. I serve this with whole grain toast, homemade jam, three slices of thick bacon and extra cream.

***Nutritional Value Per Serving:***

| | | | |
|---|---|---|---|
| 510 Calories | 20 g Fat (4 g Saturated) | 11 g Protein | 78 g Carbohydrate |
| 8 g Fiber | 245 mg Sodium | 10 mg Cholesterol | |

# The Speckled Hen Inn

**5525 Portage Road**
**Madison, WI 53704**
**(608)244-9368**
**(877)670-4844**
**www.speckledheninn.com**
**innkeeper@speckledheninn.com**

*Hosts: Patricia & Robert Fischbeck*

Escape to The Speckled Hen Inn to rest, relax, and enjoy the pleasures of a simpler life just outside one of the finest small cities in America. Stroll through the gardens or wander the woods and meadows where wildlife enjoy Mother Nature's Bed & Breakfast. Watch the sheep and llamas grazing in the pasture as you relax to your favorite music in the enclosed gazebo.

*Rates at The Speckled Hen Inn range from $109 to $169.*
*Rates include a full breakfast.*

# Farmer's Market Strata

*No summer visit to Madison would be complete without a trip to the Dane County Farmer's Market where you will find the bread, cheeses, pesto and tomatoes for this special Sunday morning treat.*

Serves 6

| | |
|---|---|
| 1 | pound loaf of sourdough bread |
| 1/2 | pound cream cheese, cut into cubes |
| 1/2 | pound fresh mozzarella, grated or in small pieces |
| 3/4 | cup basil pesto |
| 6 | ounces very thinly sliced smoked ham |
| 1 | pound (about 3 medium) red-ripe tomatoes, thinly sliced |
| 5 | large eggs |
| 1-1/2 | cups light cream or half-and-half |
| 1/2 | teaspoon salt |
| | freshly ground black pepper |

1 large mixing bowl
1 deep 2.5 quart baking dish
electric slicer is helpful but not necessary

**Baking Time: 50-55 minutes**
**Baking Temperature: 350°**

Oil or butter the baking dish. Slice the bread into 1/2-inch thick slices. Arrange 2 to 3 equal, alternating layers of the bread, cheeses, pesto, ham, and tomatoes in the baking dish. Cut or tear bread slices if needed to make complete layers.

In a large mixing bowl, whisk the eggs with the cream, salt and pepper. Pour this mixture over the layers in the baking dish. Cover and refrigerate overnight. Remove the strata from the refrigerator 20 to 30 minutes before baking. Bake until puffed and brown and set in the center. Serve garnished with a spoonful of sour cream and fresh basil leaves, if available.

*Nutritional Value Per Serving:*

| | | | |
|---|---|---|---|
| 911 Calories | 49 g Fat (22 g Saturated) | 41 g Protein | 77 g Carbohydrate |
| 5 g Fiber | 1865 mg Sodium | 279 mg Cholesterol | |

# The Audubon Inn

**45 North Main Street**
**Mayville, WI 53050**
**(920)387-5858**
**www.auduboninn.com**
**audubon@auduboninn.com**

*Host: Cindy Andrawes*

xperience the romance of an 1896 historical landmark Victorian Inn that blends today's comfort and conveniences with the captivating charms of the past. Voted one of America's "Top 54 Great Inns" by National Geographic Traveler magazine, The Audubon is a historic boutique Inn and fine dining destination renowned for gourmet food. Our 3 1/2 stars multiple award-winning on-site restaurant features freshly prepared American regional cuisine. All elegantly appointed rooms and suites include private double whirlpool baths, four poster beds, cable television, handmade quilts, sitting area and much more! Breakfast is included in your stay.

*Rates at The Audubon Inn range from $119.50 to $199.50.*
*Rates include a continental plus breakfast.*

# Audubon Inn Almond Joy Tart

*This wonderful dessert will tempt the taste buds of your guests! This sinfully sweet tart is not difficult to prepare but your guests will think you worked for days! A must make dessert to delight anyone with a sweet tooth!*

Serves 8

**Crust:**
- 1 cup graham cracker crumbs
- 1/2 cup toasted crushed almonds
- 1/4 cup sugar
- 1/4 cup melted butter

**Filling:**
- 1/2 cup canned coconut cream
- 3 ounces imported white chocolate, chopped
- 1/4 cup sour cream
- 1/4 cup (1/2 stick) unsalted butter, cut into pieces, room temperature
- 1-1/4 cups lightly packed shredded sweetened coconut

**Topping:**
- 1/4 cup whipping cream
- 3 Tablespoons unsalted butter
- 2 Tablespoons light corn syrup
- 4 ounces bittersweet (not unsweetened) chocolate, chopped
- 2 ounces imported white chocolate, chopped, melted

9" tart pan with removable bottom
heavy small saucepan
1 medium mixing bowl
parchment cone

Baking Time: 10 minutes
Baking Temperature: 350°

**Crust:**

Preheat oven to 350°. Mix together all ingredients and press mixture firmly into bottom and up sides of tart pan with removable bottom. Bake for 10 minutes. Cool on rack.

**Filling:**

Bring coconut cream to a simmer in heavy small saucepan. Reduce heat to low. Add white chocolate and stir until melted. Pour into medium mixing bowl. Whisk in sour cream. Add butter and whisk until butter melts and mixture is smooth. Stir in coconut. Chill until filling is very cold but not set, about 1 hour. Spoon filling into crust; smooth top. Chill until set.

**Topping:**

Bring first 3 ingredients to simmer in heavy saucepan, stirring frequently. Reduce heat to low. Add bittersweet chocolate and stir until melted. Reserve 3 Tablespoons hot topping. Pour remainder over tart, covering filling. Spread topping with back of spoon to cover filling evenly. Quickly spoon melted white chocolate into parchment cone. Pipe white chocolate in parallel vertical lines over topping, spacing evenly. To form decorative pattern, draw tip of small knife from left to right through chocolate lines. Draw knife right to left through chocolate lines. Repeat spacing evenly and alternate direction knife is moved. Remove pan sides. Cut into wedges.

### Nutritional Value Per Serving:

| | | | |
|---|---|---|---|
| 763 Calories | 64 g Fat (45 g Saturated) | 8 g Protein | 52 g Carbohydrate |
| 9 g Fiber | 107 mg Sodium | 47 mg Cholesterol | |

# Oaklawn Bed & Breakfast

**423 Technology Drive**
**Menomonie, WI 54751**
**(715)235-6155**
**(866)235-5296**
**www.oaklawnbnb.com**
**info@oaklawnbnb.com**

*Hosts: Maggie Foote & Les Popowski*

Oaklawn Bed & Breakfast is a century removed from today's hectic pace, perfect for taking a deep breath and just relaxing, yet just minutes from amenities and fun. Built by a lumber baron in 1890 as a stockfarm and training ground for racehorses, Oaklawn is a quiet oasis that offers a friendly, comfortable alternative in accommodations.

You'll be welcomed with a hot cup of tea, a favorite brew or a mellow glass of wine. Take your pick of four spacious guest rooms, each with private bath, decorated with found treasures and family heirlooms. This is country quiet, so you won't have any trouble getting a good night's sleep. The next morning, join us downstairs for that first cup of coffee, a full satisfying breakfast and lively conversation. Coming for business? Stay with us. We're within minutes of Menomonie's Industrial Park, UW-Stout, downtown and the Menomonie Airport.

While you're here, you must sit and enjoy our big screened porch; guests come back to enjoy it again and again. Plan a visit to the historic Mabel Tainter Theatre for a tour or live performance, enjoy a little antiquing, or try one of the local restaurants. The beautiful Red Cedar Trail follows the Red Cedar River, truly one of the best bicycling or walking trails in the Midwest. In the winter, it is groomed for cross-country skiing. There are six 18-hole golf courses within a 30-minute drive.

*Rates at Oaklawn Bed & Breakfast range from $89 to $96.*
*Rates include a full breakfast.*

# Egg Blossoms

*These individual "blossoms" always make an impression and they're easy. Blossoms have unlimited variations. Try different combinations of vegetables, cheeses and seasonings. Breakfast meats or seafood can be added. They also work well for a light lunch or supper.*

Serves 6

| | |
|---|---|
| 6 medium flour tortillas (can substitute corn or low carb) | 1/2 teaspoon black pepper |
| 3/4 cup chopped spinach or broccoli, fresh or frozen, drained | 6 slices cheese, Kraft American or your preference |
| | sour cream |
| 1/4 cup chopped green onion | |
| 1/4 cup diced red and/or green pepper | 1 large cup muffin pan or 6 individual soufflé cups |
| 8-9 large eggs | |
| 1/2 cup half-and-half cream or milk | 1 large mixing bowl |
| | sauté pan |
| 3 Tablespoons spinach dip or Ranch dressing | **Baking Time: 10-15 minutes** |
| 3/4 cup shredded cheese, Farmer's, Colby or Swiss | **Baking Temperature: 350°** |

Preheat oven to 350°. Spray muffin cups with nonstick cooking spray. Soften each tortilla in microwave with a damp paper towel for 20 seconds. Gently press and form soft tortilla into muffin cup to form a "bowl" for the egg mixture. Sauté spinach, chopped onion and peppers in lightly oiled pan, just until cooked.

Mix eggs, milk and spinach dip together in large mixing bowl. Pour into sauté pan. Gently stir to cook eggs. Add shredded cheese and pepper. Cook just until eggs are done and still moist. Remove from heat. Spoon egg mixture into tortilla cups. Place a slice of cheese over top of egg mixture in each blossom. Bake for 10-15 minutes or until cheese melts and tortillas are lightly browned. Check to be sure they don't overbake. They'll get too dark and crispy.

Remove from muffin cups and place onto plate. They will stand up nicely when surrounded with fresh fruit and sausage or bacon. Garnish each blossom with a dollop of sour cream, a sprinkle of paprika and green onion stem curls.

***Nutritional Value Per Serving:***

| | | | |
|---|---|---|---|
| 382 Calories | 21 g Fat (8 g Saturated) | 22 g Protein | 24 g Carbohydrate |
| 1.5 g Fiber | 647 mg Sodium | 346 mg Cholesterol | |

# Gresley House
# Bed & Breakfast

**13907 North Port Washington Road**
**Mequon, WI 53097**
**(262)387-9980**
**(888)270-3875**
**www.gresleyhouse.com**
**innkeepers@gresleyhouse.com**

*Hosts: John & Ruth Gresley*

*L*ocated on 20 acres of natural land, this 100-year-old Dutch gambrel style farmhouse provides an opportunity to relax in gracious but comfortable style. The public gathering room with a natural fieldstone fireplace is great for visiting or watching TV. There are walking paths and a pond for those who want to be close to nature as well as a three-seasons porch for those who prefer to sit and watch the animals walk by. The old red dairy barn and tile silo bring back a vision of days gone by but the lovely home with proximity to Cedarburg and Milwaukee enables visitors to have the best of the past and the present.

*Rates at Gresley House Bed & Breakfast range from $65 to $85.*
*Rates include a full breakfast.*

# Baked Eggs

*This recipe serves one person and will probably be adequate for most people when served with other breakfast items. But you can easily increase or decrease the number of eggs (and maybe the size of the dish) to suit your guest's appetite. You may want to slightly adjust other ingredients as appropriate. I always take a moment to explain the ingredients to our guests. Most enjoy knowing how the dish was prepared.*

Serves 1

1/2 **Tablespoon butter**
1/4 **cup grated Parmesan cheese** *Use the coarsest grate you can find or grate your own. I think it presents best.*
**dash of nutmeg**
2-3 **slices tomato** *I use firm Roma tomatoes because they are just the right texture and size for the dish.*
1/4 **teaspoon basil** *In season use fresh from the garden, of course.*
1-2 **links sausage** *Using brown and serve style keeps the prep time down.*

**7-inch au gratin dish**

**Baking Time: 12-14 minutes**
**Baking Temperature: 350°**

Preheat oven to 350°. Coat the bottom of the au gratin dish with butter. Sprinkle cheese over the bottom and sides of the dish. Crack the eggs into the dish. Sprinkle nutmeg over the eggs. Bake uncovered for 12-14 minutes (just until the yokes are solid). Check the eggs occasionally for bubbles that can develop in the whites.

While eggs cook, heat the sausage in a microwave according to its package instructions. When eggs are done, add the tomato slices on one end of the dish. Sprinkle basil over tomato and eggs. Cut sausage links in thirds and add the chunks to the other end of the dish.

Serve with a smile!

***Nutritional Value Per Serving:***

| | | | |
|---|---|---|---|
| 417 Calories | 32 g Fat (14 g Saturated) | 26 g Protein | 4 g Carbohydrate |
| 0.5 g Fiber | 857 mg Sodium | 479 mg Cholesterol | |

# My Friends' House
# Bed & Breakfast

**513 6th Avenue
P.O. Box 400
New Glarus, WI 53574
(608)527-3511
www.myfriendshousewi.net
myfriendshouse@tds.net**

*Hosts: Craig & Linda Foreback*

As a local historical marker, My Friends' House has a rich history. S.A. Schindler, grandson of one of New Glarus' original settlers, commissioned Claude & Starck of Madison to design and build this home. It was completed in 1911. Mr. Schindler served as New Glarus' first Village President. He later became Assistant Wisconsin State Treasurer. The families of Emil Kaeser & Fred Meyer also lived many decades in this home. These men were managers of the Pet Milk Company which operated in the village from 1910 until 1962.

On sunny mornings, rainbows created from the art glass windows dance throughout the large dining room. Guests will remember with pleasure the ever-changing themes of the bountiful breakfasts. Special and unique (and yes, even healthy) local products are always woven into the menu. The amenities are numerous at My Friends' House…those "special touches" that make you feel welcomed and valued. Your visit will end with your desiring a return visit to "Your" Friends' House!

*Rates at My Friends' House Bed & Breakfast range from $75 to $129.
Rates include a full breakfast.*

# Gloria-us Poppy Seed Cake

*This recipe was given to My Friends' House Bed & Breakfast as a special gift.
The recipe had been kept secret for a long time but given to us by our daughter's
mother-in-law on the occasion of opening our Bed & Breakfast. Thank you, Gloria,
for sharing your favorite recipe! "Pet Milk" was specifically named in the recipe.
Because My Friends' House was often referred to as the "Pet Milk House," we
believe this recipe was meant to grace our menu. This recipe makes a wonderful
breakfast bread or dessert!*

Serves 8-10

|       |                                          |
|------:|------------------------------------------|
| 3     | cups flour                               |
| 2     | cups sugar                               |
| 1-1/2 | cups oil                                 |
| 4     | eggs                                     |
| 1     | teaspoon vanilla                         |
| 1/2   | teaspoon salt                            |
| 1-1/2 | teaspoons baking soda                    |
| 1     | large can (12 ounces) PET (evaporated) milk |
| 1     | can (12 ounces) Solo poppy seed filling  |
| 1     | cup chopped walnuts                      |

1 large mixing bowl
angel food cake pan

**Baking Time: 1 hour 20 minutes**
**Baking Temperature: 350°**

Preheat oven to 350°. Mix ingredients in a large mixing bowl in the
order given. Pour mixture into an ungreased angel food cake pan (pan
will be heavy when removed from oven.) Bake for 1 hour 20 minutes. Let
cake cool for 5 minutes before removing from pan.

Slice thin and serve with whipped cream.

*Nutritional Value Per Serving:*

| | | | |
|---|---|---|---|
| 1061 Calories | 60 g Fat (10 g Saturated) | 15 g Protein | 117 g Carbohydrate |
| 2 g Fiber | 500 mg Sodium | 119 mg Cholesterol | |

# Pleasant Lake
# Bed & Breakfast

**2238 60th Avenue**
**Osceola, WI 54020**
**(715)294-2545**
**(800)294-2545**
**www.pleasantlake.com**
**plakebb@centurytel.net**

*Hosts: Richard & Charlene Berg*

Our home, overlooking beautiful Pleasant Lake, is set on 22 wooded acres that have been in the family since 1895. While our guests, you may stroll along the lakeshore or wooded paths, enjoy the lake from the canoe or paddleboat, then sit around the crackling campfire with the stars reflecting on the moonlit lake. While in the area, you may enjoy Interstate Park, live theater, and excursion train ride or just relax at one of the area's specialty coffee shops.

*Rates at Pleasant Lake Bed & Breakfast range from $109 to $139.*
*Rates include a full breakfast.*

# Jeanine's Meatless Taco Salad

*This is a simple and delicious new twist to the traditional taco salad. It's always a big hit!*

Serves 12

1 small head of lettuce
1 small head of cauliflower
1 medium red onion
1 pound bacon
2 cups mayonnaise (no substitutes)
3 Tablespoons sugar
1/4 bottle Salad Supreme
1 cup shredded Parmesan cheese
2 cups shredded Cheddar cheese
3 cups crumbled nacho chips

1 large mixing bowl
sharp knife
frying pan or microwave able bacon cooker
1 cup and 2 cup measuring cups
Tablespoon

Tear lettuce into small pieces and place in large bowl. Cut cauliflower into small flowerettes and add to lettuce. Cook bacon until crisp, then crumble and add to bowl. Slice red onion and add to bowl. Spread mayonnaise over the vegetables in bowl. Sprinkle with sugar. Sprinkle with cheeses. Sprinkle with seasoning (Salad Supreme). Top with crushed chips, then refrigerate until serving time.

Mix well just before serving.

***Nutritional Value Per Serving:***

| | | | |
|---|---|---|---|
| 681 Calories | 42 g Fat (14 g Saturated) | 21 g Protein | 58 g Carbohydrate |
| 6 g Fiber | 1528 mg Sodium | 66 mg Cholesterol | |

# The Country Rose Bed & Breakfast

**N7398 Highway 22
Pardeeville, WI 53954
(608)429-2035
countryrose1@mailstation.com**

*Host: Ruth Krueger*

The Country Rose Bed & Breakfast is a turn-of-the-century farmhouse located just outside of the village of Pardeeville. A quiet, relaxing home away from home—a nice place to have a reunion or family gathering. The home is decorated with antiques and old-fashioned lace curtains. Centrally located, the Country Rose Bed & Breakfast is a 30-45 minute drive to Wisconsin Dells, Baraboo, Madison, Columbus and Green Lake. Amish communities are also close by.

*Rates at The Country Rose range from $55 to $60.
Rates include a full breakfast.*

# Greek Omelette

*Often, I have guests that are vegetarian. This recipe is hearty and flavorful. Weight-conscious guests also enjoy this omelette.*

Serves 2

nonstick cooking spray
1/4 cup chopped onion
1/4 cup canned artichoke hearts, rinsed and drained
1/4 cup washed and torn spinach leaves
1/4 cup chopped plum tomato
1 cup cholesterol-free egg substitute
2 Tablespoons sliced, pitted olives, rinsed and drained
dash of black pepper

1 small mixing bowl
1 medium mixing bowl
nonstick omelette skillet
strainer
whisk
spatula
2 serving plates

**Cooking Time: 10 minutes**
**Cooking Temperature: medium**

Spray skillet with nonstick cooking spray. Heat skillet over medium heat until hot. Cook and stir onions for 2 minutes until tender-crisp. Add artichoke hearts, cook and stir until heated through. Add spinach and tomatoes; toss briefly. Remove from heat. Transfer vegetables to small mixing bowl. Wipe out skillet and spray with nonstick cooking spray.

Combine egg substitute, olives and pepper in a medium mixing bowl with whisk. Heat skillet over medium heat until hot. Pour egg mixture into skillet. Cook over medium heat for 5-7 minutes. As eggs begin to set, gently lift edges of omelette with spatula and tilt skillet so that uncooked portion flows underneath. When egg mixture is set, spoon vegetable mixture over half of the omelette. Loosen omelette with spatula and fold in half. Slide omelette onto serving plate.

**Nutritional Value Per Serving:**

| | | | |
|---|---|---|---|
| 138 Calories | 5 g Fat (1 g Saturated) | 16 g Protein | 7 g Carbohydrate |
| 2 g Fiber | 320 mg Sodium | 1 mg Cholesterol | |

# B.L. Nutt Inn

**632 East Main Street**
**Plymouth, WI 53073**
**(920)892-8566**
**www.bbinternet.com/blnutt**
**blnutt@execpc.com**

*Host: Dan Buckman*

This Italianate style home was built in 1875 of cream city brick. Ben and Sara Nutt retired here and held many social gatherings at the home. The Inn offers a front and side porch, dining room, parlor and reading room. Two guest rooms and semi-private bath are located on the second floor. East Lake furnishings adorn the home, which is located in a quiet residential area.

*Rates at B. L. Nutt Inn range from $95 to $125.*
*Rates include a full breakfast.*

# Grandma's French Toast with orange sauce and marsala cream

*The orange sauce and marsala cream add a touch of elegance to an old family favorite.
Quick and easy to prepare, this recipe will soon become a favorite of guests and hosts alike.*

Serves 6

*Batter:*
- 6 eggs
- 1/2 cup milk
- 1/4 cup Bisquick baking mix
- 2 Tablespoons sugar
- 1 teaspoon vanilla
- 1 teaspoon cinnamon
- 1/2 teaspoon nutmeg

*Orange Sauce:*
- 1 cup fresh orange juice
- 1-1/2 Tablespoons cornstarch
- 2 Tablespoons (1/4 stick) unsalted butter
- 1/4 cup sugar
- 1 Tablespoon grated orange peel

*Cream:*
- 1 cup chilled whipping cream
- 2 Tablespoons powdered sugar
- 2 Tablespoons sweet marsala

- 12 slices French bread or cinnamon/raisin bread, sliced 1" thick

- 1 large mixing bowl
- 2 medium mixing bowls
- griddle

*Toast:*
Combine batter ingredients. Dip slices of bread in batter and fry on a lightly buttered griddle, about 3 minutes per side.

*Orange Sauce:*
Whisk juice and cornstarch in bowl until cornstarch dissolves. Melt butter in heavy small saucepan over medium-high heat. Whisk in sugar, orange peel and orange juice mixture. Whisk until sauce boils and thickens slightly, about 4 minutes. Remove from heat and cool. (Can be made 2 days ahead. Cover and chill. Bring to room temperature before serving).

*Cream:*
Beat whipping cream and sugar together in medium mixing bowl until soft peaks form. Mix in marsala.

### Nutritional Value Per Serving:

| 318 Calories | 12 g Fat (6 g Saturated) | 9 g Protein | 43 g Carbohydrate |
|---|---|---|---|
| 1 g Fiber | 154 mg Sodium | 232 mg Cholesterol | |

# Gilbert Huson House Bed & Breakfast Inn

**315 Collins Street**
**Plymouth, WI 53073**
**(920)892-2222**
**gilberthusonhouse@execpc.com**
**www.husonhouse.com**

*Host: Glen Kazmierski*

*Come as Guests, Leave as Friends*

The Gilbert Huson House is a fine example of Stick Style Queen Anne Victorian architecture. Susan and Gilbert with their three children called this home, and the home remained in the family until the 1940s. In the 1980s, renovations began, and in 1988 the home was designated a county landmark and subsequently opened as a Bed & Breakfast. It is currently Sheboygan County's oldest operating Bed & Breakfast. Enjoy the comforts of our elegant Victorian home and fine guest rooms.

Six well appointed guest rooms await your arrival in this beautifully restored 1891 Victorian home. Located in the heart of Plymouth, you are within walking distance to many restaurants, shops and antiquing. We're only minutes away from Road America, Kohler and the Wade House.

*Rates at Gilbert Huson House range from $85 to $250.*
*Rates include a full breakfast.*

# Huson Egg Strata

*This delicious, easy recipe will satisfy any appetite. Prepare the dish the night before and enjoy a fabulous breakfast the next morning!*

Serves 6

1 **pound shredded hash browns**
7 **eggs**
1 **cup milk**
3 **cups shredded cheese**
  **chopped onion/green pepper/red pepper to taste**
2 **cups cubed ham (can also use bacon or sausage)**

**1 large mixing bowl**
**9" x 13" baking pan**

**Baking Time: 1 hour 15 minutes**
**Baking Temperature: 350°**

Spray baking pan with nonstick cooking spray. Cover the bottom of the pan with hash browns. Layer in order ham, cheese and veggies over the hash browns. In a large mixing bowl, whip the eggs and milk together and pour evenly over contents in the pan. Cover and refrigerate overnight.

Preheat oven to 350°. Bake for 1 hour covered. Uncover and bake an additional 15 minutes. Take out of oven and let stand for 10 minutes. Cut and serve.

**Nutritional Value Per Serving:**

| | | | |
|---|---|---|---|
| 648 Calories | 41 g Fat (18 g Saturated) | 39 g Protein | 30 g Carbohydrate |
| 3 g Fiber | 1389 mg Sodium | 345 mg Cholesterol | |

# Hillwind Farm
# Bed & Breakfast Inn

**N4922 Hillwind Road
Plymouth, WI 53073
(920)892-2199
(877)892-2199
www.hillwindfarm.com
info@hillwindfarm.com**

*Hosts: Kim & Art Jasso*

Our Bed & Breakfast was rated one of "Ten Dream Weekend Escapes" by *Milwaukee Magazine*. Enjoy the gorgeous views and romantic sunsets. This lovingly restored Victorian features five rooms with whirlpools, fireplaces, outside porches, TV/VCR/cable, CD stereos and luxurious beds. Evening wine and cheese, homemade sweet treats and much more will make your stay even more pleasurable. A stay like no other!

*Rates at Hillwind Farm Bed & Breakfast range from $94 to $184.
Rates include a full breakfast.*

# Hillwind Farm's Taco Cheese and Chile Egg Bake

*This recipe is a guest favorite and could not be easier. We serve this entrée with fresh fruit and baking powder biscuits.*

Serves 8

|   |   |
|---|---|
| 3 | cups shredded Sargento taco cheese |
| 1 | small can (4 ounces) mild, diced green chiles |
| 6 | cherry tomatoes (or a handful) |
| 14 | eggs |
| 1/2 | cup milk |
| 8 | Tablespoons butter |

**9" x 13" glass baking dish**

**Baking Time: 40-45 minutes**
**Baking Temperature: 375°**

Sprinkle 1-1/2 cups cheese over bottom of baking dish. Break eggs evenly over cheese. Break yolks with fork. Sprinkle chilies over eggs. Cut cherry tomatoes in half and sprinkle over chilies. Sprinkle remaining cheese over all. Drizzle milk over top. Cut up butter into small chunks and place evenly over all. Bake for 40-45 minutes. Let cool for 10 minutes. Cut into equal portions.

***Nutritional Value Per Serving:***

| | | | |
|---|---|---|---|
| 429 Calories | 35 g Fat (18 g Saturated) | 23 g Protein | 5 g Carbohydrate |
| 0.5 g Fiber | 574 mg Sodium | 454 mg Cholesterol | |

# Port Washington Inn

**308 West Washington Street
Port Washington, WI 53074
(262)284-5583
www.port-washington-inn.com
info@port-washington-inn.com**

*Hosts: Rita & Dave Nelson*

The Port Washington Inn provides serenity, elegance and comfort, gracious hospitality and peaceful privacy in a historic home built in 1903. Enjoy our views of Lake Michigan; walk to restaurants, the lakeshore, bike trails and shops. New for 2005 is a 5th guest suite on the third floor where the view is spectacular, major improvements throughout the inn and a beautiful new kitchen complete with AGA cookstove. The Port Washington Inn just keeps getting better! Come visit us!

*Rates at Port Washington Inn range from $100 to $200 .
Rates include a full breakfast.*

# Toast Toppings

*Each morning, we serve our homemade whole wheat bread (we grind the grain), lightly buttered and oven toasted. Many of our guests delight in that simple presentation, but it's always fun to have a variety of toppings to choose from! These are some of our guests' favorites:*

### Lemon Curd

This is also a great topper for blueberry bread pudding. Mix in plain yogurt for a perfect lemon yogurt. Makes 1 2/3 cups.

|       |                                              |
|-------|----------------------------------------------|
|       | **zest of 1 lemon**                          |
| 2/3   | **cup sugar**                                |
| 5     | **large egg yolks**                          |
| 1/2   | **cup lemon juice**                          |
|       | **pinch of salt**                            |
| 1     | **stick (1/2 cup) unsalted butter, melted and hot** |

**Food processor**
**small stainless steel saucepan**

Using a vegetable peeler, remove thin layer of lemon peel; add to sugar and process in food processor until zest is as fine as sugar. Add egg yolks, lemon juice and salt; process briefly to blend. With processor running, slowly pour melted hot butter through feed tube. Pour the mixture into saucepan and cook over low heat, stirring constantly with a wooden spoon until mixture is thickened. Do not let mixture boil at any time. Cool, cover and refrigerate. Keeps 2-3 months in a covered jar in the refrigerator.

*Nutritional Value Per Serving:*

| 109 Calories | 8 g Fat (4 g Saturated) | 1 g Protein | 10 g Carbohydrate |
|--------------|-------------------------|-------------|-------------------|
| 0 g Fiber    | 23 mg Sodium            | 86 mg Cholesterol |             |

### Honey Butter

Whip together equal portions of your favorite honey and softened butter; serve at room temperature.

### Strawberry Cream Cheese

Using softened cream cheese, add chopped sweetened fresh strawberries or your favorite strawberry preserves and mix well. May be made one day ahead and refrigerated.

# Breese Waye
# Bed & Breakfast

**816 MacFarlane Road**
**Portage, WI 53901**
**(608)742-5281**
**www.breesewaye.com**
**partridges@breesewaye.com**

*Hosts: Ray & Karen Partridge*

*E*njoy being pampered in our 1880s historic home built by the first Secretary of State of Wisconsin. Affordable luxury, Victorian elegance, warm hospitality, and lavish breakfasts await you. Within easy driving distance of Wisconsin Dells, Baraboo, two ski areas and Madison, Breese Waye Bed & Breakfast offers an experience with the spirit of yesteryear and the comforts of today!

*Rates at Breese Waye Bed & Breakfast range from $75 to $85.*
*Rates include a full breakfast.*

# Pears With Cream and Caramel

*The perfect way to start off a fall or winter morning, these pears offer a rich and old-fashioned taste. You may even serve them as a dessert, spooned over ice cream or frozen yogurt.*

Serves 4-8

    4 firm, ripe pears, peeled, halved and cored
  1/4 cup butter
  1/4 cup packed brown sugar
  1/4 cup pear liquor or pear nectar
  1/2 cup whipping cream
      dried cranberries and/or toasted pecans as
      garnish

      10" inch baking dish
      1 small saucepan

      Baking Time: 30-40 minutes
      Baking Temperature: 350°

Preheat oven to 350°. Place pears, flat side down, in lightly oiled baking pan. In small saucepan, melt butter. Add brown sugar and pear liquor or pear nectar. Stir until sugar is dissolved. Pour over pears; coat well. Bake for 20 minutes, basting frequently.

Remove from oven. Pour whipping cream over pears. Continue baking for 10-15 minutes. Serve in individual bowls, spooning sauce over pears. Add garnish, if desired.

***Nutritional Value Per Serving:***

| 278 Calories | 13 g Fat (7 g Saturated) | 1 g Protein | 42 g Carbohydrate |
| 5 g Fiber | 99 mg Sodium | 36 mg Cholesterol | |

# Lavina Inn
# Bed & Breakfast

**325 Third Street**
**Reedsburg, WI 53959**
**(608)524-6706**
**(608)727-2200 (evenings)**
**www.lavinainn.com**
**info@lavinainn.com**

*Hosts: Lorinda Broughton & Michael Manning*

*L*avina Inn is a charming turn-of-the-century Victorian home located in the historic district of Reedsburg. Guests always enjoy the rocking chairs on the large wraparound porch. The interior of this gracious home features hardwood floors, original chandeliers, unique leaded glass windows and woodwork. The home is decorated with eclectic furnishings and antique toys. Special dietary needs are addressed. Special places to visit include American Players Theater, 400 Bike Trail, Frank Lloyd Wright's Taliesin, House on the Rock, and Wisconsin Dells and Baraboo attractions.

*Rates at Lavina Inn Bed & Breakfast range from $80 to $85.*
*Rates include a full breakfast.*

# Potato & Tofu Sauce

*This sauce is delicious on wilted spinach or stir fry. You don't have to be a vegetarian to enjoy the great flavors. You will have enough for a second day to try on your other favorite vegetables!*

Serves 3-4

1 **large red potato (yields about 1 cup when cubed)**
1/2 **cup tofu**
1 **Tablespoon olive oil**
1 **Tablespoon lemon juice**
1 **can (4 ounces) mild chiles with juices (use hot chiles, if desired)**
2 **cloves garlic**
**salt & pepper to taste**

**blender or food processor**
**measuring cups**
**measuring spoons**
**small saucepan**

Boil the potato with skin on until done. When cool enough, peel off the skin and cube the potato. Place in blender. Add olive oil, lemon juice and chiles. Process until smooth. Add tofu in small size pieces and blend. Add garlic cloves and process until mixture is smooth. Salt and pepper to taste.

Place sauce in a small oven-proof dish or ramekin and warm in a hot water bath. Do not boil the sauce. Warm only the amount you need. Refrigerate covered for 3 days. Place ramekin or dish on center of dinner plate and arrange wilted spinach or favorite vegetable around it.

***Nutritional Value Per Serving:***

| | | | |
|---|---|---|---|
| 92 Calories | 5 g Fat (1 g Saturated) | 4 g Protein | 9 g Carbohydrate |
| 1 g Fiber | 118 mg Sodium | 0 mg Cholesterol | |

# Parkview
# Bed & Breakfast

**211 North Park Street
Reedsburg, WI 53959
(608)524-4333
www.parkviewbb.com
info@parkviewbb.com**

*Hosts: Tom & Donna Hofmann*

Tom and Donna Hofmann opened Parkview Bed & Breakfast in June 1989 and have enjoyed welcoming guests to Reedsburg and the area. Central to many activities, such as biking the 400 and Elroy/Sparta Trails, state parks, American Players Theatre, Taliesin, House on the Rock and Wisconsin Dells attractions, guests have no problem finding things to do. Donna, a home economist, enjoys finding new and seasonal recipes to serve the guests as part of her full, homemade breakfast.

*Rates at Parkview Bed & Breakfast range from $78 to $95.
Rates include a full breakfast.*

# Blueberry Buttermilk Oatmeal Pancakes with orange syrup

*This recipe has been used for many years and is a favorite, especially of cyclists, at Parkview Bed & Breakfast. Donna, a home economist, encourages guests to try the orange syrup instead of the traditional maple syrup. Guests are pleasantly surprised at how well the orange syrup complements the blueberry pancakes!*

Makes 12 pancakes

*Pancakes:*
- 1-1/4 cups old-fashioned oatmeal (not instant)
- 2 cups buttermilk
- 2 eggs, beaten
- 1 cup flour
- 1 Tablespoon sugar
- 1 teaspoon baking soda
- 1 teaspoon baking powder
- 1 teaspoon salt
- 1/4 cup oil
- 1-1/2 to 2 cups blueberries, fresh or frozen
- 1 teaspoon orange zest (optional)

*Orange Syrup:*
- 1-1/2 cups orange juice, fresh preferred
- 2 Tablespoons corn starch
- 3/4 cup sugar
- 1/4 cup butter
- 1 Tablespoon lemon juice, fresh preferred
- 2 teaspoons orange zest (grated orange peel)

2 medium mixing bowls
1 4-cup microwaveable bowl
measuring cups and spoons
griddle

**Cooking Temperature: 350°**

*Pancakes:*

Mix oatmeal and buttermilk. Add beaten eggs and oil. Combine dry ingredients and mix them into the oatmeal mixture. Gently stir in blueberries. Add orange zest, if desired.

Cook on a hot (350°), greased griddle until bubbles show through. Flip and cook on other side until golden brown.

*Orange Syrup:*

Combine orange juice, corn starch and sugar in a 4-cup microwaveable measure or bowl. Microwave until thickened (3-5 minutes), stirring several times. Add butter, lemon juice and orange zest. Stir until butter melts. Serve over pancakes.

***Nutritional Value Per Serving:***

| | | | |
|---|---|---|---|
| 298 Calories | 10 g Fat (3 g Saturated) | 6 g Protein | 47 g Carbohydrate |
| 2 g Fiber | 383 mg Sodium | 47 mg Cholesterol | |

# Lamb's Inn
# Bed & Breakfast

**23761 Misslich Road**
**Richland Center, WI 53581**
**(608)585-4301**
**www.lambs-inn.com**
**lambsinn@mwt.net**

*Hosts: Dick & Donna Messerschmidt*

*L*amb's Inn is located in a beautiful valley, surrounded by perennial flower beds, a large spring with a restored gazebo, a pond and small streams. Guests can relax on the enclosed porch, with an early cup of coffee. Our breakfast often features pecan waffles with a fresh peach caramel sauce, quiches, stuffed French toast with fresh strawberries or homemade bread pudding. Fresh muffins or breads and fruit complete the meal. Our inn is located 23 miles from Spring Green. We also have a cottage available.

*Rates at Lamb's Inn Bed & Breakfast range from $90 to $250.*
*Rates include a full breakfast (in the Bed & Breakfast).*

# Delectable Kringles

*Delectable kringles are versatile and can be varied by different fillings. It is very easy to make even though the recipe might look time consuming. I make the dough ahead of time and bake it before breakfast. I usually serve this on Sunday mornings as a final treat. It looks beautiful, and the guests feel they have had a special sweet to finish their breakfast.*

Serves 10

*Kringle:*
- 1 pound margarine, softened
- 4 cups flour
- 4 egg yolks
- 1 cup sour cream at room temperature
- 1 package dry yeast
- 1/2 can (21 ounce can) pie filling sliced almonds, optional

*Glaze:*
- 1/2 cup powdered sugar, without lumps
- 2 Tablespoons melted butter
- 1 Tablespoon milk
- 1/2 teaspoon vanilla or almond extract

*Mix all ingredients until smooth.*

1 large mixing bowl
1 medium mixing bowl
large cookie sheet

**Baking Time: 20 minutes**
**Baking Temperature: 375°**

*Kringle:*

In a large mixing bowl, cut margarine into the flour until it starts to stick together in clumps. In a medium mixing bowl, mix egg yolks, sour cream and yeast together. Add to the flour mixture, stir and turn out on a floured surface. Knead several times until it forms a ball. Divide the ball into 4-6 balls. Wrap each ball in Saran Wrap and refrigerate for 8 hours or overnight because the dough is very soft. It will keep for several days in the refrigerator.

In the morning, preheat oven to 375°. Roll out dough quickly on a floured surface, approximately 2 inches longer than the cookie sheet. Quickly place dough on cookie sheet. Place pie filling sparingly down the middle; fold ends up and the long sides one over the other. Let stand for 15 minutes at room temperature. Bake for 20 minutes or until golden brown. Cool. Drizzle with glaze and sprinkle with sliced almonds.

***Nutritional Value Per Serving:***

| | | | |
|---|---|---|---|
| 633 Calories | 46 g Fat (18 g Saturated) | 8 g Protein | 48 g Carbohydrate |
| 2 g Fiber | 454 mg Sodium | 140 mg Cholesterol | |

# Brownstone Inn

**1227 North 7th Street**
**Sheboygan, WI 53081**
**(920)451-0644**
**(877)279-6786**
**www.brownstoneinn.com**
**brwnstninn@aol.com**

*Host: Frank Ribich, Jr.*

*E*xperience the elegance of yesteryear in our fabulous 1907 inn. Five splendid rooms, each with its own statement, will pamper your desires with whirlpool baths, fireplaces, four-poster beds, and porches. From the grandeur of the ballroom to the magic of the billiard room, you will find yourself surrounded by the finest woods, custom marble and tile, leaded glass, sculptured ceilings and oriental rugs.

You'll also enjoy the area's attractions—Lake Michigan is a few blocks away—as well as our festivals, the Art Center, Kohler's famous golf courses, the world renowned Road America and great restaurants. Come share the past with us at the Brownstone Inn.

*Rates at the Brownstone Inn start at $175.*
*Rates include a continental plus breakfast.*

# Red Raspberry Bread

*This is a relatively quick and easy recipe that our guests really enjoy. You can substitute strawberries or blueberries for red raspberries. This makes two loaves, so you can freeze one.*

Makes 2 medium loaves

| | |
|---|---|
| 3 | eggs |
| 3 | cups flour |
| 1 | teaspoon baking soda |
| 1 | teaspoon salt |
| 3 | teaspoons cinnamon |
| 2 | cups sugar |
| 2 | packages (10 ounces each) frozen sweetened red raspberries, thawed |
| 1-1/4 | cups vegetable oil |
| 1-1/4 | cups chopped pecans |

1 small mixing bowl
1 large mixing bowl
2 medium (8"x 4") loaf pans

**Baking Time: 1 hour**
**Baking Temperature: 350°**

Preheat oven to 350°. Grease 2 loaf pans. In a small mixing bowl, beat eggs slightly. Set aside. In a large mixing bowl, stir together flour, baking soda, salt, cinnamon and sugar. Make a well in the center. Pour eggs, raspberries with their juice, and oil in center of well; mix just until moistened. Fold in pecans. Pour into two prepared loaf pans. Bake for 1 hour or until wooden toothpick inserted in center comes out clean.

*Nutritional Value Per Serving:*

| | | | |
|---|---|---|---|
| 354 Calories | 20 g Fat (2 g Saturated) | 4 g Protein | 43 g Carbohydrate |
| 3 g Fiber | 190 mg Sodium | 32 mg Cholesterol | |

# English Manor Bed & Breakfast

**632 Michigan Avenue
Sheboygan, WI 53081
(920)208-1952
(800)557-5277
www.english-manor.com
englman@excel.net**

*Hosts: Susan & William Hundley*

*L*ose yourself to romance, tranquility and European elegance the minute you walk through the doors of the English Manor Bed & Breakfast. This enchanting 1908 English Tudor has five unique guest rooms, all with fireplaces and king size whirlpools. Three additional fireplaces offer guests relaxing retreats. After your savory breakfast, stroll the lovely English gardens, or walk to the shore of beautiful Lake Michigan. Return for tea time served in our garden tea room. Enjoy a wine and cheese social in our private billiard room before dining at one of Sheboygan's exceptional restaurants. Guest pampering is foremost at the English Manor, so you will leave relaxed and rejuvenated, having arrived as a guest you will leave as a friend.

*Rates at English Manor Bed & Breakfast range from $149 to $199.
Rates include a full breakfast.*

# Heart Healthy Garden Frittata

*My guests are always surprised when I serve this frittata when they request a low fat entrée—it tastes too indulgent! It is so versatile that you can use whatever vegetables are in season, without losing taste. To round out the low fat menu, I complement this frittata with a fresh fruit cup and homemade seven grain bread (so savory that no butter is necessary). Great for lunch or dinner with a tossed salad and fresh fruit sorbet.*

Serves 6

|  |  |
|---|---|
| canola oil cooking spray | 12-inch nonstick heavy skillet |
| 2 large Wisconsin potatoes | nonstick wide spatula |
| 2 medium zucchini | cutting board |
| 2 medium yellow squash | 1 medium mixing bowl |
| 8 ounces mushroom caps | wire whisk |
| 1 medium Vadalia onion | measuring spoons |
| 1 medium green bell pepper | sharp knife |
| 1 medium red bell pepper | vegetable peeler |
| 16 ounces "Better Than Eggs" egg substitute | |
| 16 ounces low fat, finely shredded Wisconsin Cheddar cheese | |
| No-Salt and pepper to taste | |

Spray skillet with cooking spray. Wash and pat dry potatoes, finely slice and cover bottom of skillet. Wash and pat dry zucchini and yellow squash, finely slice and place over potato slices. Rinse mushroom caps, slice in half and layer over zucchini and squash. Remove outer layer from onion, slice thinly and layer over mushrooms. Wash green and red bell peppers. Use vegetable peeler and core peppers. Thinly slice peppers and layer over onion.

Place covered skillet on large burner on medium heat. Heat for 20 minutes. Pour "Better Than Eggs" into medium mixing bowl. Whisk well. Pour over layers of vegetables. Sprinkle cheese evenly over mixture in skillet. Season with No-Salt and pepper to taste. Continue to heat covered for another 20 minutes or until cooked thoroughly. Use spatula to divide frittata into 6 sections. Serve each section on fine china.

***Nutritional Value Per Serving:***

| | | | |
|---|---|---|---|
| 292 Calories | 8 g Fat (4 g Saturated) | 32 g Protein | 24 g Carbohydrate |
| 5 g Fiber | 776 mg Sodium | 17 mg Cholesterol | |

# Lake View Mansion Bed & Breakfast, Inc.

**303 St. Clair Avenue
Sheboygan, WI 53081
(920)457-5253
www.lakeviewmansion.com
lakeviewmansion@hotmail.com**

*Hosts: Renee & Richard Suscha*

*L*ake View Mansion Bed & Breakfast, Inc., is the only lodging facility in Sheboygan overlooking Lake Michigan. It offers panoramic views of the Sheboygan Marina, Yacht Club, and North Beach. The mansion is only a 10-minute drive from the championship golf courses of The Bull, Blackwolf Run and Whistling Straits, host of the 2004 PGA championship. All five guest rooms have a spectacular view of Lake Michigan, private bathrooms and king-size beds. The Bed & Breakfast has more than 10,000 square feet, featuring 11 fireplaces and a beautiful veranda overlooking Lake Michigan. Guests are always surprised by the large number of common areas they have access to on the first floor, along with the gorgeous gardens in the yard.

*Rates at Lake View Mansion range from $159 to $299.
Rates include a full breakfast.*

# Baked Oatmeal

*This quick and easy breakfast can be complemented with a side of French vanilla ice cream smothered with strawberries and bananas. Guests frequently enjoy this sumptuous breakfast in our sunroom overlooking Lake Michigan, or curled up in front of one of our 11 fireplaces!*

Serves 4

2 eggs, lightly beaten
1-1/2 cups quick cooking oats
1/2 cup sugar
1/2 cup milk
1/4 cup vegetable oil
1/4 cup chopped nuts
1/4 cup golden raisins
1 teaspoon baking powder
1/2 teaspoon salt
1/2 teaspoon ground cinnamon
1/4 teaspoon nutmeg

1 large mixing bowl
4 crocks or one 8"inch square baking dish

**Baking Time: 25 minutes**
**Baking Temperature: 350°**

Preheat oven to 350°. Combine all ingredients in large mixing bowl. Pour mixture into 4 greased crocks or a square baking dish. Bake for 25 minutes. Enjoy!

*Nutritional Value Per Serving:*
466 Calories  24 g Fat (3 g Saturated)  10 g Protein  57 g Carbohydrate
4 g Fiber  464 mg Sodium  108 mg Cholesterol

# Sheboygan Haven
# Bed & Breakfast

**W1681 Garton Road**
**Sheboygan, WI 53083**
**(920)565-3853**
**(800)595-1009**
**www.sheboyganhaven.com**
**shebhaven@powercom.net**

*Hosts: Lori & Ron Olson*

Come to the country and enjoy our 1875 farm house with antiques and a wine cellar. We are four miles from Kohler's 3 world famous golf courses: Whistling Straits, Irish Course and Blackwolf Run. Play our own 9-hole golf course. We're also just 12 miles from Road America. The shops at Woodlake, the Kettle Moraine Forest and antique mall are also nearby.

*Rates at Sheboygan Haven Bed & Breakfast range from $99.50 to $149.50.*
*Rates include a full breakfast.*

# Puff Peach Pancake

*This is a dish that our family has enjoyed for many years, easy to make and good to eat. Our guests say it tastes like a cinnamon coffee cake.*

Serves 4

*Pancake:*
- 6 eggs
- 1 cup milk
- 1 cup flour
- 1/3 cup sugar
- 1/8 teaspoon salt
- 1 teaspoon almond extract
- 1 bag (16 ounces) frozen peaches, thawed
- 7 Tablespoons butter

*Topping:*
- 1/2 cup sugar
- 1/2 cup pecan pieces
- 1/2 teaspoon cinnamon

*Mix together in small bowl.*

1 small mixing bowl
1 large mixing bowl
2-1/2 quart baking dish or 10" frying pan

**Baking Time: 30 minutes**
**Baking Temperature: 375°**

Preheat oven to 375°. Brush baking dish or deep frying pan with butter. Use wire whisk to beat eggs. Mix in milk, flour, sugar, salt and almond extract. Heat baking dish in oven with 6 Tablespoons butter to melt. Add peaches to heat, and pour batter over peaches. Sprinkle topping over batter and bake.

*Nutritional Value Per Serving:*

| | | | |
|---|---|---|---|
| 797 Calories | 39 g Fat (14 g Saturated) | 17 g Protein | 98 g Carbohydrate |
| 4 g Fiber | 357 mg Sodium | 376 mg Cholesterol | |

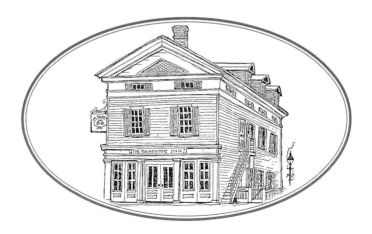

# Rochester Inn

**504 Water Street**
**Sheboygan Falls, WI 53085**
**(920)467-3123**
**www.rochesterinn.com**
**info@rochesterinn.com**

*Hosts: Sean & Jacquelyn O'Dwanny*

Rochester Inn is a beautifully restored Inn featuring spacious two-story suites. Enjoy a first floor living room and second story bedroom and bath with inviting whirlpool bath. Located one mile from the village of Kohler.

*Rates at the Rochester Inn range from $99.50 to $169.50.*
*Rates include a full breakfast.*

# Banana Bread

*Your guests and family will enjoy this delicious recipe from our Inn. Banana bread is always a welcome addition to any breakfast or brunch.*

Makes 1 small loaf and 1 regular loaf

8 **Tablespoons (1 stick) butter at room temperature**
2/3 **cup granulated sugar**
2 **eggs**
1 **cup unbleached all-purpose flour**
1 **teaspoon baking soda**
1/2 **teaspoon salt**
1 **cup whole wheat flour**
3 **large ripe bananas, mashed**
1 **teaspoon vanilla extract**
1/2 **cup chopped walnuts**

2 **medium mixing bowls**
1 **regular (9"x 5"x 3") loaf pan**

**Baking Time: 50-60 minutes**
**Baking Temperature: 350°**

Preheat oven to 350°. Grease loaf pan. Cream butter and sugar until light and fluffy. Add eggs one at a time, beating after each addition. Sift all-purpose flour, baking soda and salt together in separate bowl. Stir in whole wheat flour. Add dry mixture to wet mixture. Fold in mashed bananas, vanilla and walnuts. Pour mixture into prepared pan. Bake for 50-60 minutes or until cake tester comes out clean. Cool in pan for 10 minutes, then cool on rack.

*Nutritional Value Per Serving:*

| | | | |
|---|---|---|---|
| 175 Calories | 8 g Fat (3 g Saturated) | 3 g Protein | 24 g Carbohydrate |
| 1 g Fiber | 179 mg Sodium | 37 mg Cholesterol | |

# Inn On Maple

**414 Maple Drive**
**Sister Bay, WI 54234**
**(920)854-5107**
**www.innonmaple.com**
**innonmaple@dcwis.com**

*Hosts: Louise & Bill Robbins*

*W*e are celebrating our tenth year of welcoming guests to the historic Inn On Maple, located in the heart of Sister Bay. Here, comfortable antique-appointed accommodations, warm hospitality and delightful breakfasts are enjoyed by our guests!

*Rates at Inn On Maple range from $85 to $105.*
*Rates include a full breakfast.*

# Blueberry Croissant Puff

*This delicious recipe is easy to prepare and delicious! You can easily cut this recipe in half.*

Serves 10

4 large croissants, cut into pieces
1-1/2 cups fresh or frozen blueberries
1 package (8 ounces) cream cheese, warmed to room temperature
2/3 cup sugar
2 eggs
1 teaspoon vanilla
1-1/4 cups milk
powdered sugar
maple syrup (optional)

10 ramekins, 1/2 cup size, or 9-inch baking dish
1 medium bowl
1 electric mixer

**Baking Temperature: 350°**
**Baking Time: 20-25 minutes**

Preheat oven to 350°. Place croissant pieces evenly in 10 ramekins or across bottom of 9-inch baking dish. Sprinkle with blueberries.

Beat cream cheese, sugar, eggs and vanilla in medium bowl with electric mixer until well blended. Gradually add milk, beating until smooth. Pour evenly over croissant pieces. Let stand for 20 minutes. Bake at 350° for 20-25 minutes or until set in centers and golden brown.

Serve warm, sprinkled with powdered sugar. May be served with maple syrup.

*Nutritional Value Per Serving:*

286 Calories    15 g Fat (9 g Saturated)    6.5 g Protein    31 g Carbohydrate
1 g Fiber    297 mg Sodium    94 mg Cholesterol

# Sweetbriar
# Bed & Breakfast

**102 Orchard Drive**
**Sister Bay, WI 54234**
**(920)854-7504**
**www.sweetbriar-bb.com**
**info@sweetbriar-bb.com**

*Hosts: Mavis & Bob Arnold*

A bit off the beaten path and just far enough from town-center to provide a quiet respite from our hustle-bustle world, Sweetbriar Bed & Breakfast and its embracing meadows provide the ultimate refuge to rejuvenate mind, heart and spirit. Colonial Cape Cod architectural and decorating accents of our quiet country manor reflect the laid-back ambience of the ever-popular Northern Door peninsula, with its miles of shoreline, its numerous breath-taking state, county and town parks, its opportunities to enjoy a wide range of performing and visual arts, and its nearly never-ending variety of restaurants and specialty shops. Luxurious accommodations, including in-room fireplaces and private baths with double whirlpool tubs, sumptuous breakfasts and the warm, generous hospitality provided by innkeepers Bob and Mavis leave guests feeling ultra pampered and eagerly anticipating their next visit.

*Rates at Sweetbriar Bed & Breakfast range from $120 to $189.*
*Rates include a full breakfast.*

# Quick-'n-Easy Cherry Crescents

*These great-tasting rolls make a perfect accompaniment to our first-course fresh fruit plates. Bob loves to serve them because they're super easy to prepare, our guests rave over their delicate taste and light, flaky texture, and he gets to enjoy the occasional leftovers.*

Makes 8 breakfast-size rolls or 16 tea-time, half-size rolls

3 **Tablespoons brown sugar, loosely packed**
1 **Tablespoon butter**
1 **Tablespoon finely ground pecans**
1 **Tablespoon cherry sprinkles***
1 **package (tube) Pillsbury Crescent Dinner Rolls**
  **powdered sugar**

*\*very finely chopped (1/16" or less) dried cherries. If you can't find it at your local store, try calling Country Ovens, Forestville, WI at (920)856-6767.*

**1 small mixing bowl**
**cookie sheet**

**Baking Time: 11-13 minutes**
**Baking Temperature: 375°**

Preheat oven to 375°. In a small mixing bowl, heat butter until just melted. Add sugar, ground pecans, and cherry sprinkles, and mix to a uniform, paste consistency. Separate crescent roll triangles per package instructions and butter each with 1/8 of the cherry paste mixture. (As an accompaniment for afternoon tea, make smaller rolls by cutting the dough triangles in half and spreading 1/16 of the cherry paste mixture on each). Roll up the triangles and form into crescents, with filling on the inside.

Bake on cookie sheet for 11-13 minutes, or until golden brown. Allow to cool until the crescents are warm, sprinkle with powdered sugar and serve.

*Nutritional Value Per Serving:*

| | | | |
|---|---|---|---|
| 56 Calories | 2.5 g Fat (1 g Saturated) | 0.5 g Protein | 8.5 g Carbohydrate |
| 0.5 g Fiber | 31 mg Sodium | 5 mg Cholesterol | |

# The Franklin Victorian Bed & Breakfast

**220 East Franklin Street
Sparta, WI 54656
(608)366-1427
(888)594-FVBB
www.franklinvictorianbb.com
innkeeper@franklinvictorianbb.com**

*Hosts: Jennifer & Steve Dunn*

*A great outdoors destination with 4-seasons of recreation.*

Escape to The Franklin Victorian Bed & Breakfast in Sparta, "The Bicycling Capital of America." The Inn is located in the heart of Wisconsin's Hidden Valleys of Southwestern Wisconsin. It is a place so quiet and beautiful, it's no wonder we call it God's Country. Our celebrated rivers, rugged hills, scenic farms, tranquil back roads, bike trails, crystal air and friendly people combine to make Sparta the ideal place to find rest and renewal.

The warmth of our romantic retreat welcomes you at the door. Built in the early 1900s by a Sparta banker, Mr. W.G. Williams, this Queen Anne-style Victorian home features leaded stained glass window, fireplaces, open staircase, original woodwork, and unique architectural features.

*Rates at The Franklin Victorian range from $80 to $120.
Rates include a full breakfast.*

# Easy Wild Rice Quiche

*This is a one-bowl dish. It is easy and is my guests' favorite dish. I serve it with muffins or coffee cake, breakfast meats, seasonal fruits and beverages. This can also be made the night before and put into the refrigerator. This dish can also be vegetarian by leaving out the bacon pieces.*

Serves 6-8

        6   **eggs**
        1   **can (10 3/4 ounces) cream of**
            **mushroom soup (not diluted)**
        1   **package (2.3 ounces) Hormel or Oscar**
            **Mayer real bacon bits/pieces (use in**
            **recipe as is, do not cook)**
        1   **Tablespoon dry onion flakes**
      1/4   **teaspoon salt**
      1/4   **teaspoon pepper**
    1-1/2   **cups shredded Sharp Cheddar cheese**
        1   **cup cooked wild rice, drained**

            **1 medium mixing bowl**
            **electric mixer**
            **spatula**
            **quiche baking dish**

            **Baking Time: 35-40 minutes**
            **Baking Temperature: 350°**

Preheat oven to 350°. In a medium mixing bowl, beat eggs. Add remaining ingredients. Mix only until blended; do not over mix. Pour into quiche baking dish that has been sprayed with nonstick cooking spray. Bake uncovered for 35-40 minutes.

Garnish with orange slices and mint leaves, if desired.

***Nutritional Value Per Serving:***

341 Calories     23 g Fat (10 g Saturated)   20 g Protein      14 g Carbohydrate

2 g Fiber        917 mg Sodium               247 mg Cholesterol

# Justin Trails
# Bed & Breakfast Resort

**7452 Kathryn Avenue**
**Sparta, WI 54656**
**(608)269-4522**
**(800)488-4521**
**www.justintrails.com**
**info@justintrails.com**

*Hosts: Don & Donna Justin*

Justin Trails Resort is your center for recreation, relaxation and romantic atmosphere set in a private valley surrounded by hardwood forests. Lodging is provided in cabins and suites with a whirlpool and fireplace. Recreate with 18-basket disc golf, Nordic skiing, snowshoeing, hiking trails, bird watching and strolling through the gardens. Don and Donna Justin have been offering award-winning lodging and recreation for nearly 20 years.

*Rates at Justin Trails range from $125 to $350.*
*Rates include a full breakfast.*

# Dried Fruit Soup

*This recipe is so easy! It only requires the use of a crock pot. It's great when fresh fruit is not readily available. Serve it for breakfast, or it's luscious on ice cream. The house smells great when this is cooking!*

Serves 4

| | |
|---|---|
| 1 | quart fresh squeezed apple cider |
| 2 | teaspoons small pearl tapioca |
| 8 | ounces mixed tropical dried fruit |
| 12 | ounces dried mince meat |
| 8 | ounces dried cranberries |
| 2 | sticks cinnamon |
| 2 | whole nutmeg |

crock pot
teaspoon

**Cooking Time: 2-3 hours**
**Cooking Temperature: Low setting**

Pour all ingredients in crock pot. Mix together. Heat for 2-3 hours until tapioca pearls are soft. Stir occasionally until desired thickness. Serve warm with granola and vanilla yogurt. A loaf of French bread goes nicely with the soup.

*Nutritional Value Per Serving:*

| | | | |
|---|---|---|---|
| 965 Calories | 16 g Fat (4 g Saturated) | 16 g Protein | 196 g Carbohydrate |
| 18 g Fiber | 830 mg Sodium | 65 mg Cholesterol | |

# Hill Street
# Bed & Breakfast

**353 West Hill Street**
**Spring Green, WI 53588**
**(608)588-7751**
**www.Hillstreetbb.com**
**Hillstbb@execpc.com**

*Hosts: Kelly & Jay Phelps*

We welcome you to our 1900 Queen Anne Victorian home with handcrafted woodwork. Our guests can relax in our two living rooms and on our front porch. Guests can conveniently browse through the town's shops and art galleries then explore the area attractions. Frank Lloyd Wright's Taliesin, House on the Rock and the American Player Theater present the finest in classical theater. Recreational activities abound, such as championship golf, bicycling, canoeing and hiking in the state parks.

*Rates at Hill Street Bed & Breakfast range from $80 to $90.*
*Rates include a full breakfast.*

# Apple French Toast

*Now that we are celebrating our 10-year anniversary, we are happy to share with you one of our guests' favorite recipes. We love it because you make it the night before and bake it the next morning. We serve it with maple syrup and bacon with fresh fruit on the side. Enjoy!*

Serves 8

**French Toast:**
- nonstick cooking spray
- 10-12 wheat rolls, depending on size
- 8 large eggs
- 2 cups 2% milk
- 1/3 cup maple syrup
- 8-10 apples, Macintosh or Granny Smith

**Streusel:**
- 1/2 cup brown sugar
- 1 Tablespoon cinnamon
- 1/2 teaspoon nutmeg
- 1/4 cup flour
- 2 Tablespoons butter

1-9" x 13" baking pan
1 large mixing bowl with spout
1 small mixing bowl
whisk
peeler
knife
aluminum foil

**Baking Time: 55-60 minutes**
**Baking Temperature: 375°**

**French Toast:**

Spray pan with nonstick cooking spray. Tear wheat rolls to cover bottom of pan. In large mixing bowl with spout, whisk together eggs, milk and maple syrup. Pour over wheat rolls and push rolls down to cover with liquid. Peel and core apples and cut into slices. Arrange apple slices over wheat rolls. Sprinkle streusel over apple slices. Cover with foil and refrigerate overnight. Take out of refrigerator 1/2 hour before baking. Bake at 375° for 55-60 minutes. Uncover halfway through baking.

Let sit after removing from oven. Cut into 8 pieces and serve with maple syrup.

**Streusel:**

In a small mixing bowl, combine all ingredients until the mixture resembles coarse crumbs. Sprinkle over apples as directed above.

**Nutritional Value Per Serving:**

| | | | |
|---|---|---|---|
| 438 Calories | 12 g Fat (4 g Saturated) | 13 g Protein | 73 g Carbohydrate |
| 6 g Fiber | 271 mg Sodium | 224 mg Cholesterol | |

# The Inn On Main Street, LLC

**2141 Main Street**
**Stevens Point, WI 54481**
**(715)343-0373**
**(866)491-4010**
**www.innonmainstreet.com**
**kathysinn@charter.net**

*Hosts: Kathy & Ron Schwarz*

eel the warmth and coziness of this 1922 Lannon stone Federal Revival home of the second president of Normal School, Stevens Point. Located across from 'Old Main' building of the UWSP, we are within walking distance of campus and our historic downtown area. There is a full range of activities available, from antiquing local shops, bike riding the beautiful Green Circle trails, golf a flower hole at one of the many golf courses, to kayaking or fishing the scenic Wisconsin River or just plain relaxing under the deck umbrella with a good book.

Whatever you choose to do, we want you to feel as if it was made just for you. From the comfort of cozy guest rooms, the delectable breakfast in the morning, to the relaxation of cheese and wine in the evening, the Inn On Main Street awaits you.

*Rates at The Inn On Main Street range from $50 to $70.*
*Rates include a full breakfast.*

# Prysnac – Egg & Cheese Bake

*This dish is very versatile! It can be served to guests that are gluten intolerant or have celiac disease, or it can be "bammed" with additional ingredients such as crumbled bacon or chopped ham. You can add or subtract ingredients to fit everyone's needs.*

Serves 6

|       |                                                                                     |
|------:|-------------------------------------------------------------------------------------|
| 12    | ounces small curd cottage cheese                                                    |
| 3     | eggs                                                                                 |
| 1/4   | cup melted butter                                                                   |
| 1     | package (10 ounces) frozen chopped spinach, thawed, drained and squeezed dry        |
| 3     | Tablespoons flour (omit for gluten intolerant guests)                               |
| 1     | can (4 ounces) mushrooms, drained                                                    |
| 1-1/2 | cups grated Cheddar cheese                                                           |

1 deep dish pie plate
1 large mixing bowl
hand mixer

**Baking Time: one hour**
**Baking Temperature: 350°**

Preheat oven to 350°. Beat eggs slightly. Add cottage cheese to eggs and mix. Add the drained spinach along with the melted butter, flour (if using), mushrooms and grated cheese. Mix thoroughly. Pour into deep pie plate sprayed with nonstick cooking spray.

Bake for one hour uncovered.

*Nutritional Value Per Serving:*

| | | | |
|---|---|---|---|
| 323 Calories | 23 g Fat (12 g Saturated) | 22 g Protein | 9 g Carbohydrate |
| 2 g Fiber | 651 mg Sodium | 165 mg Cholesterol | |

# A Victorian
# Swan on Water

**1716 Water Street**
**Stevens Point, WI 54481**
**(715)345-0595**
**(800)454-9886**
**www.bbinternet.com/victorian-swan**
**victorianswan@charter.net**

*Host: Joan Ouellette*

Comfort, good food and good conversation have been our motto since 1986. Located within blocks of Stevens Point's historic downtown, this central Wisconsin bed & breakfast affords a choice of many indoor and outdoor activities. Hike, bike or ski the Green Circle Trail, which surrounds our city or canoe or kayak the Plover River that meanders around much of the same area. Great golf courses including Sentry make their home here. Antique shops and art galleries are within walking distance. Or relax in our 1889 Victorian with its original wood-work that provides guests with a chance to experience that ambience of another less stressful time.

*Rates at A Victorian Swan on Water range from $75 to $150.*
*Rates include a full breakfast.*

# A Victorian Swan
# Turtle French Toast with brandy sauce

*This has been my signature dish since 1986 with variations over the years. It can be made the night before or ahead of time and frozen, held in the oven for tardy guests and changed to accommodate guests with special likes and needs, all without losing any of its appeal.*

Serves 4-6

**French Toast:**
- 1 loaf French bread (under 1 pound)
- 4 ounces cream cheese, room temperature
- 1 teaspoon vanilla
- 2 Tablespoons sugar
- 4 Tablespoons coarsely chopped pecans
- 3 eggs
- 1/2 cup milk
- 1/3 cup chocolate chips (can be miniature)
- oil for frying

**Brandy Sauce:**
- 1 stick butter
- 1 pound brown sugar
- 1 cup whipping cream
- 1 Tablespoon brandy

1 small mixing bowl for stuffing
1 large mixing bowl for dipping mix
large fry pan for frying
9" x 13" or larger pan for holding in oven

Blend cream cheese, vanilla, nuts and sugar. Slice end off loaf. Make the next slice about 1/2 inch thick, without slicing through to the bottom and then completely slice off the next 1/2 inch thick piece. This provides you with a pocket in the middle where you will spread about a Tablespoon of cheese mixture in each pocket or as much as you like. Throw in a couple of chocolate chips on top of cheese mixture. At this point, you can freeze the toast for future use. Mix eggs, milk and a little sugar. Dip the stuffed bread and let it soak in the mixture for a few minutes. Fry until golden brown. Serve with brandy sauce. Add a couple of whole pecans for presentation. All ingredients and amounts can be changed or modified for taste or presentation. Toast can be held in oven at 170° for up to 1/2 hour.

*Brandy Sauce:*

Mix together all ingredients and slowly heat over very low heat until it boils. Cook for about one minute or two. Remove from heat and add brandy. Makes about 2 cups. Any leftovers can be refrigerated in a covered glass jar and reheated in the microwave.

**Nutritional Value Per Serving:**

| | | | |
|---|---|---|---|
| 719 Calories | 29 g Fat (14 g Saturated) | 9 g Protein | 108 g Carbohydrate |
| 1.5 g Fiber | 223 mg Sodium | 200 mg Cholesterol | |

# The Black Walnut
# Bed & Breakfast

**454 North 7th Avenue**
**Sturgeon Bay, WI 54235**
**(920)743-8892**
**www.blackwalnut-gh.com**

*Hosts: Mary & Jeff Serafico*

The House of Seven Gables is what our home was called by local residents years ago. Now named after the regal "black walnut" trees that tower over the front lawn, it has 9 gables and 4 guest rooms. Wonderful tall ceilings, angled spaces and rooflines incorporated into 4 distinctly styled rooms make our guest home a unique getaway. Double whirlpools, fireplaces, private baths and wet bars are amenities included in all suites to enhance your relaxing vacation. Our delicious homemade continental breakfast is also included, delivered to your door each morning.

Exhilarating beauty and countless activities abound in Door County in summer as well as winter. Sharing our home and love of the county with you would be our pleasure.

*Rates at The Black Walnut Bed & Breakfast range from $110 to $145.*
*Rates include a continental plus breakfast.*

# Rhubarb Pecan Muffins

*Technically, rhubarb is a vegetable, but it is cooked and eaten as a fruit. I believe rhubarb is one of the most underrated and overlooked fruit/vegetable. Its pleasant tartness is delicious by itself but also scrumptious when combined with strawberries or oranges. This recipe does that and is always a favorite in early summer when served with fresh strawberries, oranges or bananas.*

Makes 6-8 muffins

2 cups flour
3/4 cup sugar
1-1/2 teaspoons baking powder
1/2 teaspoon baking soda
1 teaspoon salt
3/4 cup chopped pecans
1 egg
1/4 cup vegetable oil
2 teaspoons grated orange peel
3/4 cup orange juice
1 teaspoon vanilla
1-1/4 cups chopped fresh or frozen rhubarb

1 medium mixing bowl
1 large mixing bowl
muffin tin

**Baking Time: 25-30 minutes**
**Baking Temperature: 375°**

Preheat oven to 375°. Remove leaves and roots (stems) from rhubarb stalks and rinse. Chop rhubarb into bite-size (1/4"-1/2") pieces. Grate orange peel. In a medium mixing bowl, combine flour, sugar, baking powder, baking soda, salt and pecans. Set aside.

In a large mixing bowl, combine egg, oil, orange peel, orange juice and vanilla. Add dry ingredients to this mixture; stir just until moist. Stir in rhubarb. Fill greased muffin tins 3/4 full. Bake for 25-30 minutes.

*Nutritional Value Per Serving:*

| 458 Calories | 20 g Fat (2 g Saturated) | 7 g Protein | 64 g Carbohydrate |
| 3 g Fiber | 628 mg Sodium | 35 mg Cholesterol | |

# Garden Gate
# Bed & Breakfast

**434 North Third Avenue**
**Sturgeon Bay, WI 54235**
**(920)743-9618**
**(877)743-9618**
**www.gardengateb-b.com**
**romance@gardengateb-b.com**

*Host: Robin Vallow*

Enjoy romantic elegance in our 1890 Victorian home surrounded by gardens and furnished with fine antiques. Garden Gate is located just two blocks from Sturgeon Bay's historical downtown with its many galleries, museums, antique shops and waterfront. Breakfast is our signature here at the Garden Gate in Door County.

*Rates at Garden Gate range from $85 to $120.*
*Rates include a full breakfast.*

# Scrumptious Chocolate Layer Bars

*This is a chocolate lover's favorite! The recipe is time-consuming but worth the effort. Chocolate and cream cheese melt together well and even better in your mouth. You'll have more than one, that's for sure!*

Makes 24 squares

**Bars:**
- 1 cup butter
- 1-1/2 cups sugar
- 2 eggs
- 1/2 teaspoon almond extract
- 1/2 teaspoon salt
- 1 teaspoon baking powder
- 3 cups flour

**Filling:**
- 2/3 cup (5.3 ounce can) evaporated milk
- 1-1/2 cups (12 ounces) semi-sweet chocolate chips
- 8 ounces cream cheese
- 1 cup walnuts
- 1/2 teaspoon almond extract

1 large mixing bowl
1 medium saucepan
9" x 13" glass baking pan

Baking Time: 35-40 minutes
Baking Temperature: 350°

**Filling:**

Melt first 3 ingredients in medium saucepan over low heat. Stir constantly until chips are melted and smooth. Remove from heat. Stir in walnuts and almond extract. Blend well and set aside.

**Bars:**

Preheat oven to 350°In large mixing bowl, combine butter, sugar, eggs and almond extract. Blend well with mixer. Add flour, salt and baking soda. Press half of mixture in greased baking pan. Spread chocolate filling on top. With remaining bar mixture, drop 1/2 teaspoonful on top of filling to create 24 evenly spaced drops. Bake for 35-40 minutes. Cool and cut into squares.

**Nutritional Value Per Serving:**

| | | | |
|---|---|---|---|
| 304 Calories | 18 g Fat (9 g Saturated) | 5 g Protein | 33 g Carbohydrate |
| 1 g Fiber | 166 mg Sodium | 50 mg Cholesterol | |

# Canyon Road Inn

**575 West Town Line Road**
**Turtle Lake, WI 54889**
**(715)986-2121**
**(888)251-5542**
**www.canyonroadinn.com**
**info@canyonroadinn.com**

*Hosts: Ken & Judy Ahlberg*

The Canyon Road Inn is a secluded lakeside getaway. Five guestrooms are featured with double whirlpools, fireplaces, king-size beds, private baths and decks or patios with lakeside views. A cottage on the lake is also available that includes two bedrooms, fireplace, sun and watercraft. Enjoy the many hiking trails and complimentary use of canoes or paddleboats. A casino is also nearby. The Canyon Road Inn has received awards from the National Bed & Breakfast contest for three years in a row!

*Rates at Canyon Road Inn range from $95 to $135.*
*Rates include a full breakfast.*

# Hash Brown Quiche

*This is an easy menu item for a wheat-free or vegetarian diet. The crust can be baked the night before, in addition to shredding the cheese and sautéing the vegetables. Just double the ingredients and place in a 9" x 13" pan for a larger group.*

Serves 4-6

*Crust:*
  3 cups frozen shredded potatoes
  1/4 cup melted butter

*Filling:*
  1 cup shredded Cheddar cheese
  1/4 cup chopped green peppers
      (other vegetables may be used,
      such as tomatoes, mushrooms,
      onions, celery or broccoli)
  4 eggs
  1/2 cup milk
  1/2 teaspoon seasoned salt

1 medium mixing bowl
pie plate or quiche baking dish

Baking Temperature:
425° for crust 350° for filling
Baking Time: 30 minutes each
for crust and filling

*Crust Preparation:*
  Preheat oven to 425°. Thaw potatoes. Line the bottom and sides of an ungreased pie plate or quiche baking dish with potatoes. Drizzle melted butter over the potatoes. Bake for 30 minutes or until lightly browned (this may be done the night before and refrigerated until morning).

*Filling Preparation:*
  Preheat over to 350°. Layer shredded cheese on top of baked crust. Top with green peppers or other vegetables. In mixing bowl, beat together eggs, milk and seasoned salt. Pour egg mixture evenly over cheese and vegetables. Bake for 30 minutes.

Cut into wedges and serve immediately.

*Nutritional Value Per Serving:*

| | | | |
|---|---|---|---|
| 467 Calories | 30 g Fat (15 g Saturated) | 20 g Protein | 31 g Carbohydrate |
| 2 g Fiber | 588 mg Sodium | 313 mg Cholesterol | |

# Walker's Barn
# Bed & Breakfast

**E1268 Cleghorn Road**
**Waupaca, WI 54981**
**(715)258-5235**
**(800)870-0737**
**www.walkersbarn.com**
**hospitality@walkersbarn.com**

*Hosts: Linda & Bob Yerkes*

Walker's Barn Bed & Breakfast is a warm, friendly, informal and relaxing country home. Come and experience the soothing peacefulness of our home nestled in the pines of central Wisconsin. Enjoy our specialty, Panne Kuechen, a delicious breakfast treat. Delight in our beautiful area where wildlife, and great shopping abound. Explore Waupaca's Chain O'Lakes and the quaint village in rural Wisconsin. We have four rooms to refresh you. Come soon! We look forward to your visit!

*Rates at Walker's Barn range from $85 to $125.*
*Rates include a full breakfast.*

# Panne Kuechen (Dutch Pancake) with maple butter topping

*Panne Kuechen is a favorite with all of our guests. You can make the maple butter ahead and refrigerate. This is a delicious recipe and well worth the extra effort.*

Serves 4

**Pancakes:**
- 4 eggs
- 3/4 cup milk
- 3/4 cup flour
- 1 Tablespoon sugar
- 1/4 teaspoon salt
- 2 Tablespoons butter or margarine

**Apple Filling:**
- 5 large Granny Smith apples- pared, cored and diced
- 2/3 cup sugar
- 1/4 teaspoon cinnamon
- 1/8 teaspoon nutmeg
- 1/3 cup butter or margarine
- 1 Tablespoon lemon juice
- 1 teaspoon lemon rind

1 medium mixing bowl
1-10" pie plate
1 medium pot
whisk

**Baking Time: 20 minutes**
**Baking Temperature: 425°**

**Pancakes:**

Preheat oven to 425°. Mix eggs, milk, flour, sugar and salt in medium mixing bowl. Batter will be thin and slightly lumpy. Melt butter in pie plate. Tilt plate to coat sides. Pour in batter. Bake for 20 minutes or until set and crust is browned. Do not open door during baking.

**Apple Filling:**

Heat butter and lemon juice. Add apples, spices and sugar. Cook until apples are tender. Serve with Panne Kuechen.

**Maple Butter Topping:**
- 1-1/2 cups sifted powdered sugar
- 1/2 cup butter or margarine, melted
- 1/2 cup maple or maple flavored syrup

Cream together powdered sugar, butter and syrup. Mix well with wire whisk. Chill and keep refrigerated until ready to serve. Serve with Panne Kuechen.

Makes 2 cups.

**Nutritional Value Per Serving:**

| | | | |
|---|---|---|---|
| 660 Calories | 28 g Fat (13 g Saturated) | 11 g Protein | 97 g Carbohydrate |
| 8 g Fiber | 389 mg Sodium | 271 mg Cholesterol | |

# Everest Inn
# Bed & Breakfast

**601 McIndoe Street**
**Wausau, WI 54403**
**(715)848-5651**
**www.everestinn.com**
**dtorkko@pcpros.net**

*Hosts: Lori & Dave Torkko*

*W*arm hospitality awaits you at our 1908 Queen Anne home. Our Bed & Breakfast offers seven spacious guest rooms furnished with antiques. A hearty breakfast, afternoon treats and a bottomless cup of coffee are a part of your stay. Relax and enjoy the wraparound sun porch, 3-season room or living room with fireplace. Conveniently located near LYW Art Museum, historic museum, downtown shopping area, churches, restaurants, Wisconsin River kayak course, and downhill and cross-country skiing.

*Rates at Everest Inn Bed & Breakfast range from $45 to $109.*
*Rates include a full breakfast.*

# Coconut Chip Coffee Cake

*Enjoy a piece of this coffee cake as part of breakfast or as a mid-day snack while sitting on our wraparound porch in the sun or by one of our fireplaces in the cool weather.*

Serves 12-16

**Cake:**
- 1/2 cup butter
- 1 cup sugar
- 2 eggs
- 1 teaspoon vanilla extract
- 2 cups flour
- 1 teaspoon baking powder
- 1 teaspoon baking soda
- 1/4 teaspoon salt
- 1 cup sour cream

**Topping:**
- 1/2 cup sugar
- 3/4 cup flaked coconut
- 1/2 cup semisweet chocolate chips
- 1/2 cup chopped walnuts

*Combine all ingredients and mix together.*

**2 large mixing bowls**
**mixer**
**bundt cake pan**

**Baking Time: 45-50 minutes**
**Baking Temperature: 350°**

Preheat oven to 350°. In a large mixing bowl, cream butter and sugar. Add eggs, one at a time, beating well after each addition. Beat in vanilla. In a separate bowl, combine flour, baking powder, baking soda and salt. Add to wet mixture, alternating with sour cream. Mix together.

Spoon half of the batter into a greased bundt pan. Sprinkle half of the topping on batter. Repeat layers and bake for 45-50 minutes.

***Nutritional Value Per Serving:***

| | | | |
|---|---|---|---|
| 454 Calories | 27 g Fat (16 g Saturated) | 6 g Protein | 50 g Carbohydrate |
| 4 g Fiber | 277 mg Sodium | 64 mg Cholesterol | |

# Rosenberry Inn
# Bed & Breakfast

**511 Franklin Street**
**Wausau, WI 54403**
**(715)842-5733**
**(800)336-3799**
**www.rosenberryinn.com**
**innkeeper@rosenberryinn.com**

*Hosts: Barry & Linda Brehmer*

The Rosenberry Inn, which also includes the 1864 DeVoe House, is located in the heart of Wausau's Andrew Warren Historic District and adjacent to the River District. Both houses have large, inviting front porches ideal for enjoying warm summer breezes and pleasant conversation. Equally relaxing is a snowy winter evening lounging in front of one of our six wood fireplaces or soaking in a double whirlpool in one of the DeVoe House suites.

*Rates at Rosenberry Inn Bed & Breakfast range from $75 to $165.*
*Rates include a full breakfast.*

# Butterscotch Pecan Breakfast Crescents

*This recipe from Linda's mother is also great with afternoon tea or coffee. The rolls are moist and fragrant and reheat well in the microwave.*

Makes 48 small rolls

*Crescents:*
- 1 package (4 ounces) butterscotch pudding
- 1-1/2 cups milk
- 1/2 cup butter
- 2 packages dry yeast
- 1/2 cup warm water
- 2 eggs
- 2 teaspoons salt
- 5 to 5-1/2 cups flour

*Filling:*
- 4 Tablespoons melted butter
- 2/3 cup brown sugar
- 2/3 cup coconut
- 1/3 cup chopped pecans

*Combine all ingredients until well mixed.*

2-quart saucepan
2-quart mixing bowl
rolling pin
2 cookie sheets

**Baking Time: 12-15 minutes**
**Baking Temperature: 375°**

Prepare butterscotch pudding according to package directions. Remove from heat and stir in butter. Cool to lukewarm temperature, stirring once or twice. Dissolve yeast in warm water and stir into cooled pudding. Beat in eggs and salt. Gradually add just enough flour to make a moderately soft dough. Turn onto floured surface and knead 5-10 minutes until dough is smooth and elastic. Place in greased bowl, turning once to grease entire surface. Let rise in warm place until double in size, about 1 to 1-1/2 hours.

Punch dough down. Divide into four parts. Cover and let rest for 10 minutes. Roll one part of the dough into a 12-inch circle. Spread 1/4 of the filling on the circle. Cut into 12 triangles. Roll each piece from the wide side to the point. Place point side down on greased cookie sheet. Let rise for about 45 minutes. Preheat oven to 375°. Bake for 12-15 minutes.

*Nutritional Value Per Serving:*

| 133 Calories | 6 g Fat (4 g Saturated) | 2.5 g Protein | 17 g Carbohydrate |
|---|---|---|---|
| 1 g Fiber | 134 mg Sodium | 17 mg Cholesterol | |

# Stewart Inn
# Bed & Breakfast

**521 Grant Street**
**Wausau, WI 54403**
**(715)849-5858**
**www.stewartinn.com**
**innkeeper@stewartinn.com**

*Hosts: Jane & Paul Welter*

Located in the historic downtown River District, this 1906 George W. Maher designed Prairie-style mansion now provides elegant lodging for visitors to Wausau. Original architectural details and fixtures preserve the craftsmanship of the era, while present-day amenities cater to the needs of today's most discerning traveler: private baths with steam showers, down comforters and pillows, Stearns & Foster mattresses, plush robes, DVD players, and wireless internet are just the beginning. Pets welcome.

*Rates at Stewart Inn range from $130 to $170.*
*Rates include a full breakfast.*

# Spinach Sausage Puffs

*Though labor intensive, this unusual entrée is well worth the effort. Carb watchers are pleased to learn that each puff has only about 20 grams of carbohydrates. Since most of the preparation can be done the night before, the morning prep is minimal. The individual servings allow flexible breakfast times and the recipe can be adjusted to serve from two to ten guests. Accompanied by a colorful fresh fruit compote and basket of warm scones, this makes a very elegant breakfast.*

Serves 6

**Puffs:**

| | |
|---|---|
| 1 | pound regular Jimmy Dean sausage |
| 1/4 | medium red onion, chopped fine (about 1/3 cup) |
| 5 | eggs, beaten |
| 1/4 | teaspoon coarse ground black pepper |
| 1/3 | cup grated Parmesan cheese |
| 1 | cup shredded Mozzarella cheese |
| 1 | package (10 ounces) frozen leaf spinach, thawed, squeezed and chopped fine nonstick cooking spray |
| 1 | cup melted butter, divided |
| 6 – 10 | sheets phyllo dough, divided (about 1 sheet per ramekin) |

**Topping:**

| | |
|---|---|
| 1 | cup small curd cottage cheese |
| 6 | Tablespoons Fischer Wieser Raspberry Chipotle Sauce |

1 large skillet
1 medium mixing bowl
scissors
wax paper
pastry brush
16-ounce Pyrex measuring cup
heavy cookie sheet
aluminum foil
6 individual (8 ounces) ramekins

**Baking Time: 45 minutes**
**Baking Temperature: 375°**

Brown sausage in large skillet until crumbly. Add onion and cook until sausage has no more pink and onion is crisp-tender. Set on wet cloth to cool. Combine eggs, pepper, cheeses and spinach in medium mixing bowl. Stir in cooled sausage mixture. Spray bottom and sides of ramekins with nonstick cooking spray. Cut wax paper circles to fit ramekins and press one circle in the bottom of each ramekin. Spray with nonstick cooking spray again.

Microwave to melt 1/3 of the butter in the Pyrex cup and brush the bottom of each ramekin with butter. Using a wax paper circle for the pattern, cut 18 phyllo dough circles. Put 3 layers in each ramekin, brushing between each layer with butter. Divide sausage/spinach mixture equally into ramekins. The ramekins should be full to the brim. Put ramekins on cookie sheet and cover with plastic wrap. Refrigerate overnight.

In the morning, preheat oven to 375°. Melt the rest of the butter and cut 42 more phyllo circles. Top each ramekin with 7 layers of phyllo, brushing between each layer and on top of the final layer with butter. Bunch the ramekins on the cookie sheet and cover loosely with a foil tent. Bake for 45 minutes, removing the foil for the last 5 minutes to brown and crisp tops. Run a knife blade around each ramekin to loosen. Carefully remove top few layers of browned phyllo and set aside. Tip ramekin onto warm plate, making sure to remove wax paper if it didn't stay with ramekin. Turn back over with a spatula and replace top phyllo layers. Microwave raspberry chipotle sauce on high for 15 to 20 seconds. Top each ramekin with about a Tablespoon of cottage cheese, then drizzle raspberry chipotle sauce (about 1 Tablespoon) over the top. Serve immediately.

## Nutritional Value Per Serving:

| | | | |
|---|---|---|---|
| 1026 Calories | 74 g Fat (31 g Saturated) | 51 g Protein | 49 g Carbohydrate |
| 16 g Fiber | 1798 mg Sodium | 336 mg Cholesterol | |

# The Little Red House Bed & Breakfast

**9212 Jackson Park Boulevard**
**Wauwatosa, WI 53226**
**(414)479-0646**
**mjwey@earthlink.net**

*Hosts: Matt & Rosemarie Wey*

The Little Red House Bed & Breakfast is an authentic Cape Cod home located in Wauwatosa, a western suburb of Milwaukee. Our location is unique: minutes from the freeways, but beautiful parks, bike trails, and a par-3 golf course are just blocks away. Mayfair Mall, fine restaurants and specialty shops are nearby. All of the Milwaukee attractions and festivals are just a short drive away.

At the end of your busy days, you'll sleep well on comfortable beds in cozy rooms, with delicious breakfasts to start your day.

*Rates at The Little Red House are $70.*
*Rates include a full breakfast.*

# Baked Oatmeal

*This is an easy recipe that can be made ahead of time and reheated. It is delicious and filling on a cold Wisconsin morning. We serve assorted fresh fruits and juice along with the oatmeal. This recipe can be easily cut in half.*

Serves 12-15

  6   **cups old-fashioned rolled oats**
  2   **cups milk**
1-1/2   **cups packed brown sugar**
3/4   **cup vegetable oil**
  4   **eggs**
  1   **teaspoon salt**
  1   **teaspoon vanilla**
      **chopped apples, raisins or coconut, optional**
      **ground cinnamon**

*Toppings:*
  **raisins**
  **milk or half-and-half cream**

  **1  large mixing bowl**
  **1-9" x 13" baking pan, sprayed with nonstick cooking spray**

  **Baking Time: 30-35 minutes**
  **Baking Temperature: 350°**

Preheat oven to 350°. Combine all ingredients in large mixing bowl, except cinnamon. Mix well. Pour into prepared baking pan and spread evenly. Sprinkle with cinnamon. Bake for 30-35 minutes or until knife inserted in center comes out clean.

May be frozen, if desired.

If you choose not to add optional apples, raisins or coconut to the main ingredients, you may choose to serve raisins on the side along with milk or cream.

*Nutritional Value Per Serving:*

| | | | |
|---|---|---|---|
| 426 Calories | 19 g Fat (2 g Saturated) | 10 g Protein | 56 g Carbohydrate |
| 4 g Fiber | 249 mg Sodium | 74 mg Cholesterol | |

# Westby House
# Victorian Inn

**200 West State Street**
**Westby, WI 54667**
**(608)634-4112**
**www.westbyhouse.com**
**info@westbyhouse.com**

*Hosts: Mike & Marie Cimino*

*Relax-Rest-Explore*

You're invited to relax and rest year round at this 1880s Queen Anne Bed & Breakfast and on-premise restaurant. Come and celebrate that special occasion or plan a getaway that will charm you with grace and elegance. Romantic bedroom chambers and Jacuzzi suites await you.

Explore the hills and valleys of Southwest Wisconsin that are filled with antiquing, shopping or one of the many recreational sports in this part of "God's country."

*Rates at Westby House range from $90 to $185.*
*Rates include a full breakfast.*

# Pineapple Cobbler

*This cobbler recipe is a classical complement to any type of brunch or teatime affair. Served warm, this is a quick and easy cobbler that your guests will savor. For variety, add diced ham or simply serve a thick-cut ham steak as the breakfast entrée.*

Serves 6

1-1/2 **cups crushed pineapple with juice**
3 **eggs**
3 **Tablespoons flour**
1 **cup sugar**
1 **Tablespoon cinnamon**
1/2 **teaspoon nutmeg**
5 **slices white bread with crust**
1/4 **pound butter**

2 **large mixing bowls**
1-9" x 9" **ovenproof dish**

**Baking Time: 30-35 minutes**
**Baking Temperature: 350°**

Preheat oven to 350°. Mix pineapple, eggs, sugar and flour together in large mixing bowl. Pour pineapple mixture into a baking dish that has been coated with nonstick cooking spray.

Melt butter and transfer to a mixing bowl. Cube bread and mix into melted butter. Add cinnamon and nutmeg.

Sprinkle bread mixture over pineapple mixture and pat down slightly. Do not mix. Bake at 350° for 30-35 minutes.

***Nutritional Value Per Serving:***

| 412 Calories | 19 g Fat (9 g Saturated) | 6 g Protein | 58 g Carbohydrate |
| 2 g Fiber | 287 mg Sodium | 146 mg Cholesterol | |

# Martha's Ethnic Bed & Breakfast

**259 East Second Street**
**Westfield, WI 53964**
**(608)296-3361**

*Hosts: Ronald & Martha Polacek*

Enjoy European hospitality and afternoon tea at Martha's Ethnic Bed & Breakfast. Rooms are Czechoslovakian, German and English. Breakfast choices are German puff pancakes with Wisconsin maple syrup, Czech crepes with fresh strawberries or English eggs and bacon with grilled tomato and broiled grapefruit. We also accommodate special diets: diabetic, low carb or low fat. We are located one block off of Hwy 51/I-39 in a picturesque small town with tree-lined streets.

*Rates at Martha's Ethnic Bed & Breakfast range from $50 to $75.*
*Rates include a full breakfast.*

# Oven Omelette

*A great tasting, very basic recipe that does not have to be refrigerated overnight. Just add any omelette ingredients that you desire. I usually add cheese and serve ham or sausage on the side.*

Serves 12

| | |
|---|---|
| 1/4 | cup butter or margarine |
| 1-1/2 | dozen eggs |
| 1 | cup milk |
| 1 | cup sour cream |
| 2 | teaspoons salt |
| 1/2 | cup chopped green onion |

1-2-quart mixing bowl
1-9" x 13" baking dish

**Baking Time: 35 minutes**
**Baking Temperature: 325°**

Preheat oven to 325°. Melt butter in baking dish to coat bottom. Beat eggs, sour cream, milk and salt together. Stir in onion and any other omelette ingredients as desired. Examples of other ingredients include cheese, ham, cooked asparagus and tomato. Bake for 35 minutes and serve immediately.

*Nutritional Value Per Serving:*

| 197 Calories | 16 g Fat (7 g Saturated) | 11 g Protein | 3 g Carbohydrate |
|---|---|---|---|
| 0.1 g Fiber | 540 mg Sodium | 337 mg Cholesterol | |

# Victoria-On-Main

**622 West Main Street
Whitewater, WI 53190
(262)473-8400
viconmain@SBCglobal.net**

*Host: Nancy Wendt*

Victoria-On-Main is an excellent example of a Queen Anne revival home built in 1895. Every room is graced with a different wood and features antiques, fine cotton with lace linens and environmentally friendly surroundings. Hike or bike in the Kettle Moraine State Forest, swim in Whitewater Lake, dine at the Fireside Dinner-Theatre or tour Old World Wisconsin.

*Rates at Victoria-On-Main range from $85 to $95.
Rates include a full breakfast.*

# Nancy's Cinnamon Scones

*These scones are a hit with just about everyone! The special ingredient is cinnamon chips, found near the chocolate chips in the grocery store. They are easy to make, and I usually have some leftovers to send home with my guests.*

Makes 18 scones

**Scones:**
- 1 cup whole wheat flour
- 2 cups white flour
- 1 Tablespoon baking powder
- 1 teaspoon baking soda
- 1 teaspoon salt
- 1/2 cup sugar
- 1 stick (8 teaspoons) butter
- 1 cup unsweetened chocolate chips
- 1/2 cup cinnamon chips
- 1/2 cup broken pecans
- 1-1/2 cups buttermilk

**Topping:**
- 1 or 2 cups confectioner's sugar
- 2 Tablespoons water (approx.)
- dash of vanilla

- 1 medium mixing bowl
- 1 pastry blender
- 1 cookie sheet

**Baking Time:** 20 minutes
**Baking Temperature:** 400°

**Scones:**

Preheat oven to 400°. Mix together both flours, baking powder, baking soda, salt and sugar. With a pastry blender, cut in butter. Stir in the chocolate chips, cinnamon chips and nuts. Add the buttermilk, stirring just until blended.

Drop by Tablespoons onto greased cookie sheet. Bake for 20 minutes.

**Topping:**

Combine all ingredients. Mixture should be a little runny. Dab topping on each scone as soon as they are removed from the oven.

**Nutritional Value Per Serving:**

| | | | |
|---|---|---|---|
| 195 Calories | 7 g Fat (3 g Saturated) | 4 g Protein | 32 g Carbohydrate |
| 3 g Fiber | 236 mg Sodium | 5 mg Cholesterol | |

**Bold type: Inns listed in this book.**

| City | Inn | Phone | Web Address |
|---|---|---|---|
| Albany | Albany House | 608/862-3636 | www.albanyhouse.com |
| | **Oak Hill Manor B&B** | **608/862-1400** | **www.oakhillmanor.com** |
| Algoma | Amberwood Inn | 920/487-3471 | www.amberwood.com |
| Alma | Gallery House B&B | 608/685-4975 | www.thegalleryhousebnb.com |
| Amery | Twin Lake Dairy B&B | 715/268-4988 ~ 888/268-3775 | www.wbba.org |
| Appleton | **Franklin Street Inn** | **920/739-3702 ~ 888/993-1711** | **www.franklinstreetinn.com** |
| | Quilt-N-Be | 920/954-0754 | www.quiltingbb.com |
| | Roost B&B | 920/882-8427 | www.theroostbandb.com |
| Arbor Vitae | Northwoods Nod-A-Way | 715/356-7700 ~ 888-NOD-A-WAY | www.wbba.org |
| Ashland | Inn at Timber Cove | 715/682-9600 | www.innattimbercove.com |
| | Residenz | 715/682-2425 | www.residenzbb.com |
| | **Second Wind Country Inn B&B** | **715/682-10** | **www.secondwindcountryinn.com** |
| Baileys Harbor | Blacksmith Inn On the Shore | 920/839-9222 ~ 800/769-8619 | www.theblacksmithinn.com |
| | **New Yardley Inn** | **920/839-9487 ~ 888-4-YARDLEY** | **www.newyardleyinn.com** |
| | Inn at Windmill Farm | 920/868-9282 | www.1900windmillfarm.com |
| Baraboo | Cranberry Cottage | 608/356-7609 | www.cranberry-cottage.biz |
| | Gollmar Guest House | 608/356-9432 | www.gollmar.com |
| | Inn at Wawanissee Point | 608/355-9899 | www.innatwawanisseepoint.com |
| | **Pinehaven B&B** | **608/356-3489** | **www.pinehavenbnb.com** |
| Bayfield | Apple Grove Inn | 715/779-9558 | www.applegroveinn.net |
| | Artesian House | 715/779-3338 | www.artesianhouse.com |
| | Cooper Hill House B&B | 715/779-5060 | www.cooperhillhouse.com |
| | Island View B&B | 715/779-5307 ~ 888-309-5307 | www.islandviewbandb.com |
| | Lucy's Place | 715/779-9770 | www.lucysplace.com |
| | **Old Rittenhouse Inn** | **888/561-4667** | **www.rittenhouseinn.com** |
| | Pilot House Inn | 715/779-3561 | www.pilothouseinn.com |
| | Pinehurst Inn at Pike's Creek | 715/779-3676 | www.pinehurstinn.com |
| | Thimbleberry Inn B&B | 715/779-5757 | www.thimbleberryinn.com |
| Belleville | **Cameo Rose Victorian Country Inn** | **608/424-6340** | **www.cameorose.com** |
| Birchwood | Cobblestone B&B | 715/354-3494 | www.cobblestonebedandbreakfast.com |
| Black Creek | Old Coach Inn B&B | 920/984-3840 | www.wbba.org |
| Blue River | **Cream Pitcher** | **608/536-3607** | **www.mwt.net~crmptchr** |
| Browntown | Honeywind Farm | 608/325-5215 | www.wbba.org |
| Burlington | **Hillcrest Inn & Carriage House** | **262/763-4706 ~ 800/313-9030** | **www.thehillcrestinn.com** |
| Cambridge | Cambridge House B&B | 608/423-7008 ~ 888/859-8075 | www.cambridgehouse-inn.com |
| | Covington Manor | 608/423-1333 | www.covingtonmanorbandb.com |
| | Lake Ripley Lodge | 877/210-6195 | www.lakeripley.com |
| Camp Douglas | Bluff View B&B | 608/427-3631 | www.wbba.org |
| | Sunnyfield Farm B&B | 608/427-3686 ~ 888/839-0232 | www.sunnyfield.net |
| Campbellsport | Inn the Kettles B&B | 920/533-8602 | www.innthekettles.com |
| Cascade | Madison Avenue Inn | 920-528-1391 | |
| Cashton | Ages Past Country House B&B | 608/654-5950 ~ 888/322-5494 | www.agespast.net |
| | Country Pleasures | 608/839-4915h ~ 608/625-2665 | www.countrypleasuresbandb.com |
| Cassville | Geiger House | 608/725-5419 ~ 800/725-5439 | www.geigerhouse.com |
| | River View B&B | 608/725-5895 ~ 888/297-5749 | www.riverviewbb.com |
| Cedarburg | Stagecoach Inn B&B | 262/375-0208 ~ 888/375-0208 | www.stagecoach-inn-wi.com |
| Chetek | Sweet Dreams B&B | 715/924-4590 ~ 800/890-0116 | www.wbba.org |
| Chippewa Falls | **McGilvray's Victorian B&B** | **715/720-1600 ~ 888/324-1893** | **www.mcgilvraysbb.com** |
| | Pleasant View B&B | 715/382-4401 | www.pleasantviewbb.com |
| Coloma | River House | 715/228-3283 | www.wbba.org |
| Columbus | Columbus Carriage House B&B | 920/623-4925 | www.columbuscarriagehouse.com |
| Cornucopia | Fo'c'sle B&B | 715/742-3337 | www.siskiwitbay.com |
| | Village Inn | 715/742-3941 | www.villageinncornucopia.com |
| Crandon | **Courthouse Square B&B** | **715/478-2549 ~ 888/235-1665** | **www.wbba.org** |
| Cross Plains | Enchanted Valley B&B | 608/798-4554 | www.enchantedvalley.com |
| Delavan | Allyn Mansion Inn | 262/728-9090 | www.allynmansion.com |
| Dodgeville | Grandview | 608/935-3261 | www.grandview.com |

| City | Inn | Phone | Web Address |
|------|-----|-------|-------------|
| Eagle | Eagle Centre House B&B | 262-363-4700 | www.eagle-house.com |
| Eagle River | **Inn at Pinewood, Inc.** | **715/477-2377** | **www.inn-at-pinewood.com** |
| East Troy | Elliott House | 262-363-9666 | www.elliotthouse.net |
| | Pickwick Inn | 262-642-5529 | www.pickwickinn.com |
| Eau Claire | Apple Tree Inn | 715/836-9599 ~ 800/347-9598 | www.appletreeinnbb.com |
| | Atrium B&B | 715/833-9045 ~ 888/773-0094 | www.atriumbb.com |
| | Otter Creek Inn | 715/832-2945 | www.ottercreekinn.com |
| Egg Harbor | Door County Lighthouse Inn | 920/868-9088 | www.dclighthouseinn.com |
| | Feathered Star B&B | 920/743-4066 | www.featheredstar.com |
| Elkhorn | Ye Olde Manor House | 262-742-2450 | www.yeoldmanorhouse.com |
| Ellison Bay | Hotel Disgarden | 920/854-9888 ~ 877/378-3218 | www.hoteldisgarden.com |
| Elroy | East View B&B | 608-463-7564 | www.eastviewbedandbreakfast.com |
| Ephraim | **Eagle Harbor Inn** | **920/854-2121 ~ 800/324-5427** | **www.eagleharbor.com** |
| | **French Country Inn of Ephraim** | **920/854-4001** | **www.wbba.org** |
| | Hillside Inn of Ephraim | 920/854-7666 | www.visitephraim.com |
| | Trollhaugen Lodge | 920/854-2713 | www.trollhaugenlodge.com |
| Fall River | **Fountain Prairie Inn** | **920/484-3618** | **www.fountainprairie.com** |
| Ferryville | Mississippi Humble Bush | 608/734-3022 | www.wbba.org |
| Fish Creek | Juniper Inn | 920/839-2629 ~ 800/218-6960 | www.juniperinn.com |
| | Thorp House Inn & Cottages | 920/868-2444 | www.thorphouseinn.com |
| | Whistling Swan Hotel | 920/868-3442 | www.whistlingswan.com |
| | White Gull Inn | 920/868-3517 | www.whitegullinn.com |
| Florence | **Lakeside B&B** | **715/528-3259** | **www.northern-destinations.com/lakeside** |
| Fort Atkinson | **LaGrange B&B** | **920/563-1421** | **www.1928barn.com** |
| | Lamp Post Inn | 920/563-6561 | www.thelamppostinn.com |
| Gill's Rock | Harbor House Inn | 920/854-5196 | www.door-county-inn.com |
| Glen Haven | Parson's Inn | 608/794-2491 | www.parsonsinn.com |
| Green Bay | Astor House | 920/432-3585 ~ 888/303-6370 | www.astorhouse.com |
| Green Lake | Carvers On The Lake | 920/294-6931 | www.carversonthelake.com |
| | **McConnell Inn** | **920/294-6430 ~ 888/238-8625** | **www.mcconnellinn.com** |
| | Miller's Daughter B&B | 920-294-0717 | www.millersdaughter.com |
| Hales Corners | Barnes House B&B | 414/525-9303 | www.wbba.org |
| Hayward | Forest Moon B&B | 715/634-5188 | www.forestmoonbb.com |
| | Mustard Seed | 715/634-2908 | www.haywardlakes.com/mustardseed |
| Hazel Green | Wisconsin House Stage Coach Inn | 608/854-2233 | www.wisconsinhouse.com |
| Hazelhurst | Hazelhurst Inn | 715/356-6571 | www.wbba.org |
| Holcombe | **Happy Horse B&B** | **715/239-0707** | **www.happyhorsebb.com** |
| Horicon | **Honeybee Inn B&B** | **920/485-4855** | **www.honeybeeinn.com** |
| Hudson | Baker Brewster Victorian Inn | 715/381-2895 ~ 877/381-2895 | www.bakerbrewster.com |
| | Escape by the Lake | 715/381-2871 | www.escapebythelake.com |
| | Jefferson-Day House | 715/386-7111 | www.jeffersondayhouse.com |
| | **Phipps Inn** | **715/386-0800 ~ 888/865-9388** | **www.phippsinn.com** |
| Hurley | Anton - Walsh House | 715/561-2065 | www.anton-walsh.com |
| Janesville | Scarlett House | 608/754-8000 | www.scarletthouse.com |
| Kendall | Cabin at Trails End | 608/427-3877 | www.mwt.net/~cabin |
| Kewaunee | Historic Norman General Store | 920/388-4580 | www.normangeneralstorebb.com |
| La Crosse | Celtic Inn | 608-782-7040 | www.wbba.org |
| | **Four Gables B&B** | **608/788-7958** | **www.bedandbreakfast.com/ppf/602305.aspx** |
| | Wilson Schoolhouse Inn | 608/787-1982 | www.wilsonschoolhouseinn.com |
| La Farge | **Trillium** | **608/625-4492** | **www.trilliumcottage.com** |
| Lac du Flambeau | Heiwausou | 715-588-7993 | |
| Lake Geneva | **General Boyd's B&B** | **262/248-3543** | **www.generalboydsbb.com** |
| | Golden Oaks Mansion | 262/248-9711 | www.goldenoaksmansion.com |
| | Lazy Cloud B&B | 262/275-3322 | www.lazycloud.com |
| | Pederson Victorian B&B | 262/248-9110 ~ 888/764-9653 | www.pedersonvictorian.com |
| | Roses B&B | 262/248-4344 ~ 888/767-3262 | www.rosesbnb.com |
| Lake Mills | Fargo Mansion Inn | 920/648-3654 | www.fargomansion.com |
| | Sweet Autumn Inn | 920/648-8244 | www.sweetautumninn.com |
| Lancaster | Maple Harris Guest House & Cottage | 608/723-4717 ~ 888/216-0888 | www.mapleharris.com |
| LaValle | Mill House on Main | 608/985-7900 | www.wbba.org |
| Lodi | Prairie Garden B&B | 608/592-5187 ~ 800/380-8427 | www.prairiegarden.com |
| | **Victorian Treasure Inn** | **608/592-5199 ~ 800/859-5199** | **www.victoriantreasure.com** |
| Lomira | White Shutters | 920/269-4056 | www.wbba.org |

| City | Inn | Phone | Web Address |
|------|-----|-------|-------------|
| Madison | **Annie's Garden B&B** | **608/244-2224** | **www.bbinternet.com/annies** |
| | Arbor House | 608-238-2981 | www.arbor-house.com |
| | Canterbury Inn | 608/258-8899 | www.madisoncanterbury.com |
| | Collins House B&B | 608/255-4230 | www.collinshouse.com |
| | Hotel Ruby Marie | 608/327-7829 | www.rubymarie.com |
| | Mansion Hill Inn | 608/255-3999 ~ 800/798-9070 | www.mansionhillinn.com |
| | Parsonage | 608/838-7383 ~ 877/517-9869 | www.parsonagebANDb.com |
| | **Speckled Hen Inn** | **608/244-9368** | **www.speckledheninn.com** |
| Maiden Rock | Harrisburg Inn | 715/448-4500 | www.harrisburginn.com |
| Manawa | Ferg Haus Inn | 920/596-2946 | http://fergsbavarianvilage.com |
| | Lindsay House B&B | 920/596-3643 | www.lindsayhouse.com |
| Manitowoc | Bedell Hill | 920/683-3842 | www.wbba.org |
| | WestPort B&B | 920/686-0465 | www.thewestport.com |
| Marinette | Lauerman House Inn | 715/732-7800 | www.mmvictorian.com |
| | M & M Victorian Inn | 715/732-9531 | www.mmvictorian.com |
| Mayville | **Audubon Inn** | **920-387-5858** | **www.audubonInn.com** |
| | J & R's Sherm Inn | 920/387-4642 | www.wbba.org |
| | River's Bend Inn | 920/387-2224 | www.riversbendinn.com |
| Mazomanie | Walking Iron B&B | 877/572-9877 | www.walkingiron.com |
| Medford | Gibson House LLC | 715/748-5019 | www.wbba.org |
| Mellen | Mellen House B&B | 715/274-9207 ~ 877/774-9207 | www.bbonline.com/wi/mellen/ |
| Menomonie | **Oaklawn B&B** | **715-235-6155** | **www.oaklawnbnb.com** |
| Mequon | American Country Farm B&B | 262/242-0194 | www.americancountryfarm-bedandbreakfast.com |
| | **Gresley House B&B** | **262/387-9980** | **www.gresleyhouse.com** |
| Merrill | Candlewick Inn | 715/536-7744 ~ 800/382-4376 | www.candlewickinnbb.com |
| Milwaukee | Acanthus Inn B&B | 414/342-9788 ~ 877/468-8740 | www.acanthusinn.prodigybiz.com |
| | Brumder Mansion B&B | 414/342-9767 | www.brumdermansion.com |
| | Knickerbocker B&B Suites | 414/276-8500 | www.knickerbockeronthelake.com |
| Mineral Point | Brewery Creek | 608/987-3298 | www.brewerycreek.com |
| | Red Shutters B&B | 608/987-2268 | www.redshutters.com |
| Minocqua | Sill's Lakeshore B&B | 715/356-3384 | www.sillslakeshorebandb.com |
| | Whitehaven B&B | 715/356-9097 | www.whitehavenbandb.com |
| Monroe | Ludlow Mansion B&B | 608/325-1219 | www.ludlowmansion.com |
| | Victorian Garden B&B | 888/814-7909 ~ 608/328-1720 | www.wbba.org |
| Mount Horeb | Arbor Rose B&B | 608/437-1108 | www.arborrosebandb.com |
| Neillsville | Tufts Mansion | 715/743-3346 | www.wbba.org |
| New Glarus | **My Friends' House** | **608/527-3511** | **www.myfriendshousewi.net** |
| New London | Antiques With Inn | 920/982-4366 | www.antiqueswithinn.com |
| Oconomowoc | Inn at Pine Terrace | 262/567-7463 | www.innatpineterrace.com |
| Oconto | Rose of Sharon B&B | 920/834-9885 | www.roseofsharonbnb.com |
| Onalaska | Lumber Baron Inn | 608/781-8938 | www.wbba.org |
| Osceola | **Pleasant Lake B&B** | **715/294-2545 ~ 800/294-2545** | **www.pleasantlake.com** |
| | St. Croix River Inn | 715/294-4248 | www.stcroixriverinn.com |
| Pardeeville | **Country Rose B&B** | **608/429-2035** | **www.wbba.org** |
| Pepin | Summer Place | 715/442-2132 | www.summerplace.net |
| Pewaukee | Quilted Decoy B&B Inn | 262/547-1699 | www.wbba.org |
| Plymouth | **B.L. Nutt Inn** | **920/892-8566** | **www.bbinternet.com/blnutt** |
| | **Gilbert Huson House** | **920/892-2222** | **www.husonhouse.com** |
| | **Hillwind Farm B&B Inn** | **920/892-2199 ~ 877/892-2199** | **www.hillwindfarm.com** |
| | Tauschek's B&B Log Home | 920/876-5087 | www.tauscheksbedandbreakfastloghome.com |
| Port Washington | **Port Washington Inn** | **262/284-5583 ~ 877/794-1903** | **www.port-washington-inn.com** |
| Port Wing | Garden House B&B | 715/774-3705 | www.garden-house.com |
| Portage | **Breese Waye B&B** | **608/742-5281** | **www.breesewaye.com** |
| | Cedar Ridge B&B | 608/429-3639 | www.cedarridgebb.com |
| Poynette | Jamieson House Inn | 608/635-4100 ~ 608/635-2277 | www.jamiesonhouse.com |
| Prairie du Chien | Neumann House B&B | 608/326-8104 ~ 888/340-9971 | www.prairie-du-chien.com |
| Prescott | Arbor Inn | 715/262-4522 ~ 888/262-1090 | www.thearborinn.com |
| Princeton | Ellison's Gray Lion Inn | 920/295-4101 | www.wbba.org |
| Reedsburg | **Parkview B&B** | **608/524-4333** | **www.parkviewbb.com** |
| | Pine Grove Park B&B | 608/524-0071 | www.pinegroveparkbb.com |
| Rice Lake | Spring Creek B&B | 715/736-2005 | www.springcreekbandb.com |
| Richland Center | **Lamb's Inn B&B** | **608/585-4301** | **www.lambs-inn.com** |
| Rio | Mill House Inn | 608/429-2195 ~ 888/682-1110 | www.millhousebandb.com |
| River Falls | Kinni Creek Lodge & Outfitters | 715/425-7378 | www.kinnicreek.com |

| City | Inn | Phone | Web Address |
|------|-----|-------|-------------|
| Sheboygan | **Brownstone Inn** | **920/451-0644 ~ 877/279-6786** | **www.brownstoneinn.com** |
| | **English Manor B&B** | **920/208-1952 ~ 877/481-0941** | **www.english-manor.com** |
| | **Lake View Mansion B&B Inc.** | **920-457-5253** | **www.lakeviewmansion.com** |
| | **Sheboygan Haven B&B** | **920/565-3853 ~ 800/595-1009** | **www.grammalori.com** |
| Sheboygan Falls | Fringe A Country Inn | 920/467-3172 | www.thefringecountryinn.com |
| | **Rochester Inn** | **920/467-3123** | **www.rochesterinn.com** |
| Siren | Lilac Village B&B | 715/349-7012 ~ 888/891-1207 | www.lilacb-b.com |
| Sister Bay | **Inn On Maple** | **920/854-5107** | **www.innonmaple.com** |
| | **Sweetbriar B&B** | **920/854-7504** | **www.sweetbriar-bb.com** |
| | Woodenheart Inn | 920/854-9097 | www.woodenheart.com |
| Soldiers Grove | Inn at Lonesome Hollow | 608/624-3429 | www.lonesomehollow.com |
| Sparta | Cranberry Country B&B | 608/366-1000 ~ 888/208-4354 | www.cranberrycountry.com |
| | **Franklin Victorian B&B** | **608/366-1427** | **www.franklinvictorianbb.com** |
| | Grapevine Log Cabins | 608/269-3619 | www.grapevinelogcabins.com |
| | **Justin Trails B&B Resort** | **608/269-4522 ~ 800/488-4521** | **www.justintrails.com** |
| | Lighthaus Inn B&B | 608-269-4002 | www.lighthausinn.com |
| | Strawberry Lace Inn | 608/269-7878 | www.spartan.org/sbl |
| Spring Green | **Hill Street B&B** | **608/588-7751** | **www.hillstreetbb.com** |
| Springbrook | Stout Trout B&B | 715/466-2790 | www.wbba.org |
| Stevens Point | Dreams of Yesteryear | 715/341-4525 | www.dreamsofyesteryear.com |
| | **Inn on Main Street** | **715/343-0373** | **www.innonmainstreet.com** |
| | **Victorian Swan On Water** | **715/345-0595 ~ 800/454-9886** | **www.bbinternet.com/victorian-swan** |
| Stoughton | Naeset-Roe Inn | 608/877-4150 | www.naesetroe.com |
| Sturgeon Bay | **Black Walnut Guest House** | **920/743-8892** | **www.blackwalnut-gh.com** |
| | **Garden Gate B&B** | **920/742-9618** | **www.gardengateb-b.com** |
| | Gray Goose B&B | 920/743-9100 ~ 877/280-4258 | www.ggoosebb.com |
| | Inn at Cedar Crossing | 920/743-4200 | www.innatcedarcrossing.com |
| | Inn The Pines B&B | 920/743-9319 | www.innthepinesbb.com |
| | Little Harbor Inn | 920/743-3789 | www.littleharborinn.com |
| | Quiet Cottage on the Lake | 920/743-4526 | www.quietcottage.com |
| | Reynolds House B&B | 920/746-9771~ 877/269-7401 | www.reynoldshousebandb.com |
| | Sawyer House B&B | 920/746-1640 ~ 888/746-1614 | www.bbonline.com/wi/sawyer |
| | Scofield House | 920/743-7727 | www.scofieldhouse.com |
| | White Lace Inn | 920/743-1105 ~ 877/948-5223 | www.WhiteLaceInn.com |
| | White Pines Victorian Lodge | 920/746-8264 or 920/559-1880 | www.whitepineslodge.com |
| | Whitefish Bay Farm B&B | 920/743-1560 | www.whitefishbayfarm.com |
| | Colonial Gardens B&B | 920/746-9192 | www.colgardensbb.com |
| Tomahawk | Eagles Rest Bed & Breakfast | 715/453-7515 | www.eaglesrest.com |
| Turtle Lake | **Canyon Road Inn, LLC** | **715/986-2121** | **www.canyonroadinn.com** |
| Two Rivers | Red Forest B&B | 920/793-1794 ~ 888/250-2272 | www.redforestbb.com |
| | Richmond's Guest Lodge | 920/794-1714 | www.richmonds.net |
| Viola | Inn at Elk Run | 608/625-2066 | www.elkrun.net |
| Viroqua | Pietsch Tree Farm | 608/634-3845 | www.peachtreefarm.com |
| Wabeno | Crystal Bell Inn B&B | 715/473-2202 | www.thecrystalbell.com |
| Washburn | Pilgrim's Rest | 715/373-2964 | www.ncis.net/pilgrimr/ |
| Waterford | River View Inn | 262/534-5049 ~ 888/534-8439 | www.bbinternet.com/riverviewinn |
| Waupaca | Beasley Lake B&B | 715/258-2000 | www.beasleylake.com |
| | Crystal River Inn | 715/258-5333~800/236-5789 | www.crystalriver-inn.com |
| | Green Fountain Inn | 715/258-5171~ 800/603-4600 | www.greenfountaininn.com |
| | **Walker's Barn B&B** | **715/258-5235 ~ 800/870-0737** | **www.walkersbarn.com** |
| Wausau | **Everest Inn** | **715/848-5651** | **www.everestinn.com** |
| | **Rosenberry Inn** | **715/842-5733** | **www.rosenberryinn.com** |
| | **Stewart Inn** | **715/849-5858** | **www.stewartinn.com** |
| Wauwatosa | **Little Red House B&B** | **414/479-0646** | **www.wbba.org** |
| West Salem | Wolfway Farm | 608/486-2686 | www.wbba.org |
| Westby | **Westby House Victorian Inn** | **608/634-4112 ~ 800/434-7439** | **www.westbyhouse.com** |
| Westfield | **Martha's Ethnic B&B** | **608/296-3361** | **www.wbba.org** |
| White Lake | Jesse's Historic Wolf River Lodge | 715/882-2182 | www.wolfriverlodge.com |
| Whitewater | Hamilton House B&B | 262/473-1900 | www.bandbhamiltonhouse.com |
| | **Victoria-on-Main B&B** | **262/473-8400** | **www.wbba.org** |
| Wilton | Rice's Whispering Pines | 608/435-6531 | www.wbba.org |
| Wisconsin Dells | Thunder Valley Inn | 608/254-4145 | www.thundervalleyinn.com |
| | Whispering Waters B&B | 608/253-8388 | www.dellswwbb.com |
| | White Rose Inns | 608/254-4724 | www.thewhiterose.com |

# Index of Recipes

## To order additional copies of

### *Cooking Inn Style - bon Appétit!*

as well as other books in the Bed & Breakfast series or for a FREE catalog contact The Guest Cottage Inc. Also, visit us online at www.theguestcottage.com

The Guest Cottage Inc.
*dba Amherst Press*

PO Box 848
Woodruff, WI 54568
voice: 800-333-8122
fax:    715-358-9456